T0305377

Concise Introduction to Organization Theory

Elgar Concise Introductions are inspiring and considered introductions to the key principles in business, expertly written by some of the world's leading scholars. The aims of the series are two-fold: to pinpoint essential principles of business and management, and to offer insights that stimulate critical thinking. By distilling the subject into a concise and meaningful form, the books serve as accessible introductions for graduate and undergraduate students coming to the subject for the first time. Importantly, they also develop well-informed, nuanced critiques of the field that will challenge and extend the understanding of advanced students, scholars and thinking practitioners.

For a full list of Edward Elgar published titles, including the titles in this series, visit our website at www.e-elgar.com.

Concise Introduction to

Organization Theory
From Ontological Differences to Robust Identities

MICHAEL LOUNSBURY

Professor of Strategy, Entrepreneurship and Management, Alberta School of Business, University of Alberta, Canada and Professor of Business Strategy & Entrepreneurship, The Australian National University College of Business and Economics, Australia

JOEL GEHMAN

Professor of Strategic Management and Public Policy and Thaddeus A. Lindner and Sergius Gambal Professor of Business Ethics, George Washington School of Business, George Washington University, USA

Elgar Concise Introductions

 Edward Elgar
PUBLISHING

Cheltenham, UK • Northampton, MA, USA

Published by
Edward Elgar Publishing Limited
The Lypiatts
15 Lansdown Road
Cheltenham
Glos GL50 2JA
UK

Edward Elgar Publishing, Inc.
William Pratt House
9 Dewey Court
Northampton
Massachusetts 01060
USA

A catalogue record for this book
is available from the British Library

Library of Congress Control Number: 2024932701

This book is available electronically in the **Elgar**online
Business subject collection
http://dx.doi.org/10.4337/9781803921273

ISBN 978 1 80392 126 6 (cased)
ISBN 978 1 80392 128 0 (paperback)
ISBN 978 1 80392 127 3 (eBook)

Printed and bound by CPI Group (UK) Ltd, Croydon, CR0 4YY

Contents

Acknowledgements   vii

1   **Introduction: the organization theory landscape**   **1**
     1.1   A brief overview of organization theory   2
     1.2   Ontological differences in contemporary
            organization theory   9
     1.3   Mapping the organization theory field   14
     1.4   The role of power in organization theory   21
     1.5   Ontology, theoretical research communities,
            and scholarly identity   22
     1.6   How the book unfolds   26

2   **Rationalist theories**   **29**
     2.1   Philosophical foundations of rationalist
            theories: utilitarianism   30
     2.2   Rational choice theories   32
     2.3   Organizational ecology   35
     2.4   Contingency theory   38
     2.5   Discussion   39

3   **Pragmatic theories**   **42**
     3.1   Philosophical foundations of pragmatist
            theories: American pragmatism   43
     3.2   Behavioral theory of the firm   45
     3.3   Resource dependence   48
     3.4   Embeddedness and networks   51
     3.5   Social movements and organizations   54
     3.6   Discussion   58

4   Co-constitutive theories   **61**
   4.1   Philosophical foundations of co-constitutive
         theories: phenomenology   62
   4.2   Institutional theory   64
   4.3   Sensemaking   70
   4.4   Practice theory   73
   4.5   Discussion   78

5   The broad reach of organization theory   **80**
   5.1   Organization theory in the study of entrepreneurship   82
   5.2   Organization theory in the field of strategy   88
   5.3   Discussion   97

6   Conclusion: building a robust scholarly identity   **99**
   6.1   Engaged scholarship and the impact imperative   100
   6.2   "Get me an organization theorist, stat!"   102
   6.3   The remaking of the public intellectual   104
   6.4   Tackling grand challenges   107
   6.5   Conclusion   114

References   116
Index   153

Acknowledgements

The development of this book has benefitted from incredibly helpful comments and suggestions from Howard Aldrich, Emily Block, Vern Glaser, Nina Granqvist, Royston Greenwood, Tim Hannigan, Bob Hinings, Markus Höllerer, David Kirsch, Nico Klenner, Saku Mantere, Renate Meyer, Birgit Muskat, Wendy Smith, Chris Steele, Nick Wang, and many other faculty and students from around the world. We are particularly grateful to our colleagues at Aalto University, the University of Alberta, Australian National University College of Business and Economics, and George Washington University for providing feedback at various stages of this project. While we mindfully considered and did our best to integrate the feedback we received (some of it very spirited), given the pluralism and diverse ontological commitments of our wider scholarly community, we hope you will understand that it was never our intention to please everyone.

1. Introduction: the organization theory landscape

Organization theory is a vibrant, multidisciplinary social science field that is centered at the interface of sociology and management, but also draws on ideas from varied disciplines including anthropology, economics, philosophy, political science, psychology, and science and technology studies. Given these diverse foundations, it is perhaps unsurprising that the field encompasses many different (sometimes conflicting) ontologies (i.e., assumptions about the nature of reality). A foundational task for emerging organization scholars is to develop their scholarly identities and position themselves within academic conversations and communities to ensure their ideas resonate. Yet, this is easier said than done. Scholars who fail to fully understand fundamental ontological differences among organization theories may inadvertently draw on ideas that are inherently contradictory, leading to conceptual confusion. To ensure ideas are understood and embraced by intended audiences (particularly reviewers), scholars must develop a nuanced understanding of theoretical differences and position their work accordingly. This is also critical to bridging ontological differences and making contributions that are relevant to diverse audiences. In short, developing theoretical contributions that are interesting and impactful requires developing a deep appreciation for how different audiences – not only scholars, but also practitioners and the public more broadly – think.

To help scholars develop such an appreciation, we ontologically distinguish organization theories along two dimensions: how they conceptualize the institutional context and how they conceptualize organizational actors. Our novel mapping of the field unpacks broad similarities and differences among organization theories, revealing the landscape within which scholarly identities are constructed and scholarly outputs are appreciated or ignored. We identify three main types of theories – rationalist, pragmatic, and co-constitutive – which are undergirded by distinctive philosophical traditions – utilitarianism, pragmatism, and phenomenology. Our typology highlights contradictions within some

1

theoretical conversations, and surfaces opportunities to bridge ontologies by engaging in scholarly conversations across our theoretical categories. Our central aim is to promote engaged scholarship and help organization theorists build robust scholarly identities, thereby enabling them to meaningfully contribute to multiple academic conversations and maximize real-world relevance – including scholarship that addresses various grand challenges (Carton, Parigot, & Roulet, 2023; Schneider, 2023).

1.1   A brief overview of organization theory

At the core of organization theory is a focus on organizations and organizing. Organizations are everywhere – they include formal organizations such as corporations, nonprofits, social enterprises, and state agencies, as well as more informal and sometimes transitory organizations that may comprise varied partnerships, workgroups, nascent entrepreneurial ventures, communal gatherings, political campaigns, and social movements. Organizations help to structure and govern social interaction and behavior; we not only work in organizations, but also interact with a multitude of organizations as we engage in our everyday routines. Organizations also have crucial impacts on society through their contributions to economic inequality, politics, and the environment (Haveman, 2022).

As Charles Perrow (1991) emphasized, the prevalence and importance of organizations, as well as the fact that *organizing* is a central process in the constitution of society and economy, is the raison d'être of organization theory. Echoing this sentiment, Mary Jo Hatch (2018: 3) argued, "we need to know as much as we can about organizing practices and processes that create our organizations and institutions if we are to make the best use of them instead of allowing them to rule us." As a field, organization theory emerged over the course of the 20th century, influenced by 19th and early 20th century social theorists such as Karl Marx, Max Weber, Emile Durkheim, and Georg Simmel, who focused on societal changes related to the rise of industrial capitalism and large scale bureaucratic organizations, as well as by classical management theorists (e.g., Barnard, 1938; Fayol, 1949 [1916]; Follett, 1918; Taylor, 1911), who focused more on how to manage these new, large organizations more efficiently and effectively (see Hinings & Meyer, 2018 for a more detailed treatment of these starting points). Tensions between these two general programs of research that emerged in the early 20th century continue to this day.

More sociological approaches to organizational analysis have remained heavily influenced by the agendas cultivated in social theory, focusing on big questions about how organizations and organizing relate to large scale societal changes, such as those associated with the dynamics of capitalism. In contrast, more managerially oriented scholars, often influenced by economic theory, have tended to approach organizations as instrumental tools created to achieve objectives. While sociological approaches to organization theory were vibrant in the 1950s and 1960s, many have argued that more economically oriented managerialist approaches became more dominant as organization theorists increasingly joined business schools and focused on developing knowledge about strategy and performance (e.g., Lounsbury & Ventresca, 2003; Stern & Barley, 1996).

Nonetheless, it is important to note that the growing importance of business and management schools in the 1950s and 1960s greatly facilitated the formalization and growth of the field of organization theory. Established in 1936, the Academy of Management is the leading professional association for management researchers in the United States, one that became more relevant to scholars interested in organization theory when it launched *Academy of Management Journal* in 1957 (Wrege, 1986), one year after the debut of *Administrative Science Quarterly* in 1956. In 1965, the *Handbook of Organizations*, edited by Jim March, was published, laying out a broad agenda for the study of organizational processes. Notably, the Organization and Management Theory (OMT) division was created within the Academy of Management in 1971, providing a core administrative apparatus for organization theory scholars. Over time, the field became more elaborated and internationalized. For instance, *Academy of Management Review* was launched in 1976; the first issue of *Organization Studies*, the journal of the European Group for Organization Studies was published in 1980; and *Research in the Sociology of Organizations*, an important outlet at the interface of sociology and management, was established in 1982.

While the shift of organization theory to business schools solidified more economically oriented managerialist approaches, it did not stymie the robust development of more sociologically rooted theories, as we document in this book (see also Haveman, 2022). Because others have already provided excellent historical overviews of the field (e.g., Hinings & Meyer, 2018; Scott & Davis, 2007), we do not rehash its origins in depth, but zoom in on contemporary theoretical conversations and debates that are central to the field's current and future development. That is, we seek to provide current scholars with a foundational touchstone to understand diverse perspectives on organizations and organizing. Our view is that organization theory scholars not only need to understand how the field has developed and which current theoretical research programs are most vibrant, but also how different theories and scholars relate to each other, as well as the opportunities these relations create for cultivating a robust scholarly identity and making novel contributions to knowledge.

We focus less attention on how to conduct research and the details of how to construct major theoretical contributions to knowledge, as many good general resources on theorizing and constructing social theory already exist (e.g., Martín, 2014; Stinchcombe, 1968; Swedberg, 2014; Weick, 1989), and scholars develop their research and theoretical contributions in myriad ways. Instead, we aim to develop an architecture of the organization theory field that clarifies how to cultivate a robust scholarly identity in a field with diverse theoretical research traditions.

A scholarly identity is one's position in the field based on the intellectual resources leveraged to undergird the theorizing process and the formulation of theoretical contributions (e.g., Stinchcombe, 1986). Theoretical resources locate a scholar in a particular theoretical conversation, thereby signaling to relevant audience(s) that the research produced may be of interest (Huff, 1999). This positioning is also reflected in citation patterns, which signal not only relevant foundational knowledge, but also the communities a scholar belongs to (or seeks to join). Scholars from these communities provide a pool of likely reviewers who will assess the quality of research for publication, including how the claimed contributions of a paper extend theoretical conversations (Locke & Golden-Biddle, 1997).

While some theoretical conversations have a large audience, others can be quite narrow and specialized. A robust scholarly identity is not only able to appeal to specialized audiences, but also capable of multivocality – appealing to multiple audiences across different theoretical research programs. This is not about popularity or politics, but publishing – the reality of getting one's scholarly ideas peer-reviewed, in print, and available to the broader academic community. Padgett and Ansell's (1993: 1263) analysis of Cosimo de' Medici highlights the enabling role of multivocality: "the fact that single actions can be interpreted coherently from multiple perspectives simultaneously." In Cosimo's case, cultivating such a robust identity created latitude for action by "maintaining discretionary options across unforeseeable futures in the face of hostile attempts by others to narrow those options" (p. 1263). It is rare for scholars to appeal to everyone in the field, given the multidisciplinary character of organization theory. That is, some theories are more complementary, while others may be antagonistic. One way of sidestepping potential hostilities is to pursue different theoretical projects across different research outputs, and then, channeling Cosimo, respond "graciously to the flow of requests" (p. 1264) that are likely to ensue (such as from disparate reviewers). Conversely, engaging multiple theories simultaneously can have downsides to the extent that scholars in different theoretical camps do not appreciate each other (Pfeffer, 1993). Worse, scholarly papers that signal reviewers from divergent theoretical camps often end up being rejected, potentially exacerbating the widespread tendency for divergence in reviewer assessments (Starbuck, 2003).

To cultivate a more robust scholarly identity across multiple audiences, we believe it is important to appreciate how explicit and implicit assumptions about the nature of the social world shape one's research in relation to other scholars. Such core assumptions are often rooted in ontological differences – that is, assumptions about the nature of being and reality – that distinguish theoretical conversations and researchers from each other. As early career scholars, both of us were inspired by a very influential book by Burrell and Morgan (1979), *Sociological Paradigms and Organizational Analysis*, which emphasized the importance of ontological assumptions in mapping the field of organizational sociology at that time. They noted that:

> Social scientists ... are faced with a basic ontological question: whether the "reality" to be investigated is external to the individual – imposing itself on individual consciousness from without – or the product of individual consciousness; whether "reality" is of an "objective" nature, or the product of individual cognition; whether "reality" is a given "out there" in the world, or the product of one's mind. (Burrell & Morgan, 1979: 1)

These broad distinctions tend to map onto realist and nominalist ontologies, respectively. Given the multidisciplinary influences in organizational theory, it is no surprise that such ontological differences exist. Indeed, a major impetus for writing this book was our sense that fewer and fewer early career scholars are being exposed to core philosophy of science ideas that undergird organization theorizing, at a time when ontological and philosophical considerations are as important as ever, if not more so (Adler, 2009; Tsoukas & Chia, 2011). This may be associated with a variety of factors, including the decline of hegemonic belief systems rooted in neoliberalism and modernity more generally (Lounsbury & Wang, 2020), as well as the growing diversity of scholars who have entered the field from around the world who bring their own scholarly traditions to bear on the study of organizations and organizing.

The field of organization theory, which became more formalized in business schools in the 1960s and 1970s, tends to have a North American bias, due, in part, to the dominance of U.S. business schools globally. However, European scholarship, which has historically tended to be influenced by different traditions that value philosophical engagement, has grown in prominence in recent decades. Increasingly, scholars from Asia, the Global South, and elsewhere have become more involved, raising critical questions about colonial influences on dominant strands of organization theory (Banerjee, 2022; Hamann et al., 2020). For instance, Indigenous scholarship provides some of the most strident challenges to dominant understandings of organization theory (Bastien, Coraiola, & Foster, 2023; Salmon, Chavez, & Murphy, 2022); some even have argued that terms such as "research" and "ontology" are simply synonyms for colonialism (Smith, 1999; Todd, 2016). Notably, some scholars are taking steps to develop an interface between organization theory and Indigenous studies that seeks to avoid the pitfalls of Western cultural imperialism (e.g., Doucette, Gladstone, & Carter, 2021; Peredo & McLean, 2013; Salmon et al., 2022).

While we are open to various views and scholarly traditions, we also believe that scholarly discourse occurs in a commons where we need to be able to understand and talk to each other. Thus, we leverage ontological differences – that is, alternative assumptions about what exists and, thus, what is available for us to study – to highlight the fruitfulness of understanding the philosophical foundations of different theoretical packages. Indeed, ontological considerations are a recurrent theme across the sciences. As Kuhn (1970) famously proposed, scientific progress is not a matter of accumulating theory-independent facts. Rather, science takes place within paradigms – worldviews that provide scholars with sets of assumptions, principles, methods, and problems. Research is a conversation that takes place within and against such paradigms, which encompass alternative ontologies and knowledge interests. In turn, scientific progress is punctuated by paradigmatic revolutions, or shifts in the dominant worldview in particular domains.

In the field of management, Morgan (1980: 606) built centrally on Kuhn's notion of paradigms, which he defined simply as "alternative realities." Going beyond Kuhn, however, Morgan (1980: 607) sought to understand the role of paradigms in social theory, the analysis of which he argued "must uncover the core assumptions that characterize and define any given worldview, to make it possible to grasp what is common to the perspectives of theorists whose work may otherwise, at a more superficial level, appear diverse and wide ranging." In this conceptualization, what Morgan (1980: 607) interchangeably referred to as "metatheoretical paradigms" and "worldviews" were superordinate to particular "schools of thought," or "different ways of approaching and studying a shared reality or worldview."

More recently, Ketokivi and colleagues (2017) complemented Morgan's insights by foregrounding the role of analogies in organization theory. In a move reminiscent of Kuhn, they rejected the possibility that "progress is defined as the accumulation of ideologically neutral, objective facts" (p. 638). Instead, they conceived of research on organizations as taking place within heterogenous research communities. Building on the notion of research programs (Lakatos, 1970), they argued that "in organizational research, progress occurs within subcommunities united by a common core analogy" (Ketokivi et al., 2017: 638). As a corollary, analogy-based theorizing betrays one's ontological positions; "the choice of the core analogy defines what the ontological position is. Saying 'I am going to think of the firm as if it were a nexus of contracts' clearly conveys an ontological commitment" (Ketokivi et al., 2017: 651).

Consistent with Kuhn, Morgan, and Ketokivi and colleagues, we argue that the ontological assumptions of some theoretical approaches can be more easily bridged than others. While we recognize that the dominant traditions at the core of this book have a Western bias, our aim is to provide a way to understand the diversity of theorizing. Alongside the notion of ontology, we surface the axiologies, or values systems, latent in different philosophies of science which are less frequently made explicit. In doing so, we seek to both explore existing axiologies and stimulate the possibility of alternative ones. Overall, our hope is that the framework we develop will facilitate several outcomes. First, and most directly, we seek to help scholars develop arguments that will be accepted by increasing the legibility and comprehensibility of their scholarly identities. Second, we invite other scholars who have an interest in organizations, but come from other traditions and forms of knowing, to engage some of the scholars and scholarship we discuss, and highlight how their approaches may provide fresh perspectives on organizations and organizing. Third, we seek to further the collective production of knowledge in the organization theory field by encouraging a plurality of ontologically infused theoretical approaches.

We pay less attention to epistemology – the branch of philosophy that focuses on what counts as knowledge and how knowledge is generated. While there is certainly an intertwined relationship between ontology and epistemology (Burrell & Morgan, 1979; Hatch, 2018), with implications for the methods and analytical approaches that scholars use (Gehman et al., 2018), most extant treatments tend to reinforce an unhelpful antinomy between quantitative and qualitative research that has become more of an ideological divide (Aldrich, 2014; Astley & Van de Ven, 1983; Kaplan, 2015). Without denying the importance of epistemology and its interrelationship with ontology, we believe that good scholarship, grounded in variegated forms of evidence (i.e., quantitative and qualitative), can be found within and across different forms of ontologically grounded theories. We encourage students to become open to understanding, if not appreciating, good scholarship in whatever form it takes. Of course, consistent with philosophers of science such as Kuhn and Lakatos, different theoretical packages may have more or less rigidity with regard to their epistemological commitments and the forms of evidence they deem credible.

In the next section, we develop a more multidimensional approach to understanding ontological differences (and possibilities for rapprochement) among organization theories. Our focus is on how organization theories conceptualize organizations in relationship to their environment. In doing so, we explicate differences among so-called open-systems theories (Scott & Davis, 2007). We discuss two key dimensions that we believe are fruitful in ontologically distinguishing main lines of organizational theorizing. One dimension focuses on how organization theories conceptualize the nature of the institutional context – their contextual emphasis – while the other concentrates on how theories conceptualize organizational actors. We leverage these dimensions to provide a novel mapping of the field of organization theory that helps to unpack broad similarities and differences among theories, providing a landscape within which scholarly identities are constructed, and scholars and their scholarly outputs are appreciated or ignored.

1.2   Ontological differences in contemporary organization theory

In the context of social science theorizing, ontology typically refers to scholars' implicit and explicit assumptions about the nature of reality and assertions about the entities that exist in or populate that reality (DeLanda, 2009; Snape & Spencer, 2003). These assumptions are typically embedded in theoretical research programs (Ketokivi et al., 2017; Lakatos, 1970), and scholars typically adopt particular ontological assumptions (sometimes unwittingly) as a result of how and by whom they were trained. In many Ph.D. programs, scant attention is paid to the philosophical underpinnings of organization theories, often resulting in a lack of reflexivity about key assumptions that drive our understanding of the world as well as the extent to which scholarly insights are paradigm-laden (Kuhn, 1970; Morgan, 1980). This can prevent scholars with divergent ontological assumptions from productively interacting or appreciating the knowledge generated by different theoretical research programs.

As we mentioned earlier, traditional discussions of ontology in organization theory tend to emphasize the distinction between realism and nominalism (Burrell & Morgan, 1979).[1] Realism refers to the philosophical position that posits the reality of the social world external to individual cognition, one which is physical, measurable, and objectively knowable in principle. This is quite common in economically oriented managerialist theories. Nominalism refers to an opposite philosophical position, wherein the social world external to individual cognition is assumed to consist of names, concepts, and labels used to structure reality. These labels are convenient but artificial. Whereas realism emphasizes abstract and general universals, nominalism emphasizes concrete and specific particulars.

In organization theory, these ontological distinctions have been paralleled by others, such as between positivism and post-positivism, determinism and voluntarism, and nomothetic and ideographic methods. They also tend to differentiate more objectivist approaches that conceptualize organizations as instrumental tools to achieve goals from those that seek to understand organizations as complex systems with multiple, potentially incompatible goals, fuzzy boundaries, and more expressive dimensions that are substantively important. But such distinctions are overly simplistic relative to the richness of organization theory. Rather than fall back on binary tropes, our aim is to highlight the importance of ontology and to develop a more multidimensional approach that enhances an understanding of the richness and diversity of organization theories and promotes constructive dialogue within and across theoretical camps.

As noted earlier, we highlight two key ontological dimensions that we believe are useful in understanding organization theory. One dimension draws attention to how theories conceptualize the nature of an organization's environment, distinguishing between theories that emphasize the importance of economic, social or cultural aspects of an organization's context. The other dimension unpacks how theories conceptualize organizational actors, distinguishing whether context is conceptualized as more exogenous or endogenous to an understanding of organizational behavior. We discuss these dimensions in turn.

1.2.1   Contextual emphasis

This dimension aims to capture the explicit or implicit theoretical assumptions about the environment or context in which an organization is situated. For instance, more managerial approaches which treat organizations as instrumental tools tend to conceptualize organizational environments as comprising economic forces, with a particular focus on how organizations access and accumulate material resources (e.g., financial capital) to survive and grow. While social relationships and cultural forces may be mentioned, they are often marginalized relative to economic forces such as supply and demand.

Contemporary managerial approaches that emphasize economic conditions and external pressures mainly aim to cultivate knowledge about how to better manage organizations. These approaches build on the legacy of contingency theorists in the 1960s who drew upon the administrative theories of Taylor, Barnard, and Fayol to identify optimal organizational designs for different environmental conditions, developing prescriptions for managers that might enhance organizational performance (e.g., Burns & Stalker, 1961; Lawrence & Lorsch, 1967; Thompson, 1967). A central concept in this line of research was the notion of *environmental uncertainty*, which was invoked to characterize how external conditions faced by an organization shape organizational behavior and outcomes (see also Duncan, 1972; Hickson et al., 1971; Pfeffer & Salancik, 1978). For instance, Duncan (1972) constructed a 2 × 2 framework that characterized organizational environments across two dimensions – simple/complex and static/dynamic – arguing that complex and dynamic environments create the most uncertainty for organizational decision-makers.

In her review of the environmental uncertainty literature, Milliken (1987) identified three main definitions: (1) an inability to assign probabilities regarding the likelihood of future events; (2) a lack of information about cause-effect relationships; and/or (3) an inability to predict the outcomes of a decision accurately. Despite differences in how environmental uncertainty is conceptualized, most managerial research focuses on profit-making firms that seek to maximize performance (often, shareholder returns), necessitating access to resources from actors external to the organization – whether they are customers or other organizations, including government agencies. Managerial approaches that conceptualize organizational environments with an emphasis on economic resources are particularly prominent in contemporary strategy research as well as various strands of organization theory.

More sociologically informed approaches to organizational analysis do not ignore the importance of economic forces and resources, but tend to conceptualize organizational environments as more multidimensional socio-cultural spaces. Some theories, such as those that employ network analysis, give primacy to social relationships, while other theories, such as those that employ institutional analysis, give primacy to cultural processes. Theories that emphasize the social or cultural nature of an organization's environment seek to highlight how the nature and impact of economic forces are crucially moderated by social and cultural processes.

As signaled earlier, these approaches to organization theory were importantly imprinted by social theorists such as Weber (e.g., 1978), whose historical and comparative approach to organizations emphasized how broader societal dynamics shaped the nature of organizing. Weberian scholarship seeded research on how wider societal institutions fundamentally shape the emergence and operations of organizations across space and time (e.g., Bendix, 1956; Stinchcombe, 1965). While managerial approaches conceptualize organizational environments in universalistic and unitary ways, sociological approaches stress the importance of understanding differences in institutional contexts across space and time, as well as differences in their pathways and trajectories.

This broader conceptualization of organizational environments lends itself to asking a wider array of questions. Instead of focusing exclusively on how organizations are able to achieve more optimal performance, sociological approaches also focus on the societally shaped identities and meanings associated with organizations, how they evolve over time, and how organizations may reshape societal institutions (Scott & Davis, 2007). In addition, sociological scholarship is more likely to study a wider array of organizational forms – for-profit, non-profit, governmental, temporary, social movements – that comprise an organization's environment.

1.2.2   Relationship of context to organizational actors

The other ontological dimension we emphasize is how organization theories connect their contextual emphasis to organizational behavior. While the first dimension focuses on the nature of an organization's environment, this dimension concentrates attention on core assumptions about how wider contexts relate to actors. In most managerial theories, and even some sociological approaches, an organization's environment is considered to be an exogenous set of forces. This was especially true of most organization theories in the 1960s and 1970s.

In their overview of the literature at the time, Astley and Van de Ven (1983) argued that there was a crucial divide between theories that emphasized organizational choice versus environmental determinism. For instance, some approaches focused on the fact that even though environmental pressures constrained organizational action, the leaders of most organizations had a range of strategic choices that they could pursue to cope with or manage these pressures (Child, 1972; March & Simon, 1958; Pfeffer & Salancik, 1978). In contradistinction, theories that adopted a more structural (Blau & Scott, 1962; Lawrence & Lorsch, 1967; Thompson, 1967; Woodward, 1965) or natural selection approach (Aldrich, 1979; Hannan & Freeman, 1977) conceptualized organizational behavior as determined, very highly constrained, or even random – managerial discretion was regarded as having little to no substantive impact on organizational effectiveness or performance. As we discuss in Chapter 2, organizational ecologists most prominently staked out this ontological position, drawing on biological ideas to develop arguments that shifts in the nature of organizational environments shape the births and deaths of entire organizational populations, as opposed to organizational performance (Hannan & Freeman, 1977).

However, many sociologists at the time sought to go beyond conceptualizing organizational environments as exogenous, instead imagining the relationship between organizations and environments as more endogenous to organizational behavior. Sociologists had long recognized that a proper analysis of organizations involved developing a deeper understanding of how organizations interact with other actors in the environment, including suppliers, buyers and regulatory agencies. For instance, in his famous study of the Tennessee Valley Authority (TVA), a federally owned utility corporation created to help poor farmers by expanding the electricity grid to rural areas, Selznick (1949) documented various interactions with external stakeholders, ultimately leading to cooptation by powerful organizations that derailed the progressive mandate that had led to the TVA's creation. Stinchcombe (1959), a student of Selznick, highlighted that while industrial production is organized primarily within corporate bureaucracies, other forms of production (e.g., craft production) tend to be organized by professionals across formal organizational structures. This opened a broader literature on how forms of organizing in occupations, professions and other types of work often crosscut corporate forms of organizing and generate conflict rooted in different sources of authority (Scott, 1965).

Building on this literature, scholars in the 1960s also began to conceptualize organizations as interconnected with other organizations in their environment via network relationships (e.g., Aiken & Hage, 1968; Evan, 1965;

Hirsch, 1972). As formal network analysis began to infiltrate organization theory in the 1970s, a more structural approach to organization theory was developed, focusing on mapping various kinds of inter-organizational relationships in industries, markets and fields (e.g., Aldrich & Whetten, 1981; Burt, 1982; Mizruchi, 1982; White, 1981). This approach rejects the notion that organizations are usefully conceived as independent entities navigating forces emanating from an external environment, viewing them instead as embedded in multiplex relationships, thereby necessitating an analysis of wider organizational fields (Granovetter, 1985).

A more radical shift towards conceptualizing environmental context as endogenous to an understanding of organizational behavior occurred with the rise of social constructivist, phenomenological and ethnomethodological approaches in the 1960s (e.g., Berger & Luckmann, 1967; Garfinkel, 1967; Goffman, 1967). While these approaches importantly brought issues of culture, meaning and perception to the fore, they often were marginalized or ignored as "subjectivist" (Burrell & Morgan, 1979); mainstream organizational scholars believed such approaches could not yield a more systematic theoretical research program. These ideas, however, greatly influenced the emergence of the new institutionalism in organizational analysis (DiMaggio & Powell, 1983; Meyer & Rowan, 1977; Powell & DiMaggio, 1991). As these more meaning-centered approaches gained currency in organization theory, the environment became more fully endogenized, and scholars began to emphasize how organizations and their environments are co-constituted (e.g., Garud, Gehman, & Giuliani, 2014; Lounsbury & Wang, 2020; Meyer & Vaara, 2020).

1.3   Mapping the organization theory field

Figure 1.1 combines these dimensions to provide an ideal-typical typological mapping of how contemporary organization theories differ ontologically. Typologies provide a fruitful way to theorize by using abstract categories to group broadly similar kinds of phenomena and by distinguishing between complex examples (Delbridge & Fiss, 2013; Doty &

Glick, 1994). Note that in any typology, the theorized categories are ideal types, as explained by Weber (1949: 90):

> an ideal type is formed by the one-sided accentuation of one or more points of view and by the synthesis of a great many diffuse, discrete, more or less present and occasionally absent concrete individual phenomena, which are arranged according to those one-sidedly emphasized viewpoints into a unified analytical construct.

Weber's (1978) ideal type of bureaucracy is exemplary, focusing on how roles and routines are enmeshed in a hierarchical structure governed by managers who apply rationalized standards. While this abstract ideal type can shed light on dynamics in many kinds of organizations, immense variation can be observed in the details and extent of bureaucracy. For instance, some organizations may embrace more communal or collegial forms of governance that seem to contradict conventional images of corporate governance.

Thus, ideal types are formed from characteristics and elements of a given phenomenon, but are not meant to correspond to all characteristics of any particular case. This implies that while we believe our categorization of ideal typical organization theories is useful for analyzing ontological similarities and differences across theories, the specific uses of theory in published studies may deviate from the categorizations we invoke. In this book, we aim to leverage this complexity to highlight how contradictions may exist within some theoretical conversations and uses of theory, and surface opportunities to bridge ontologies to the extent that scholarly conversations occur across our theoretical categories.

Given these caveats, we identify three main types of theories – rationalist, pragmatic, and co-constitutive. *Rationalist* theories tend to emphasize economic forces and conceptualize an organization's environment as exogenous. *Pragmatic* approaches tend to stress the contextual importance of social relationships and processes, and conceptualize these relational processes as intertwined with the practical-evaluative behavior of focal organizations (Emirbayer & Mische, 1998). These theories tend to conceptualize the environment as partly exogenous and partly endogenous. *Co-constitutive* perspectives alternatively emphasize the primacy of cultural processes in an organization's environment and conceptualize this context as endogenous to the nature and functioning of organizations. In addition, theories in these three categories are undergirded by distinctive philosophical traditions – utilitarianism, pragmatism, and phenomenology. While we do not extensively discuss different philosophical traditions, we emphasize their importance in ontologically grounding different strands of theorizing in deep traditions of thought, as well as their corresponding axiological commitments.

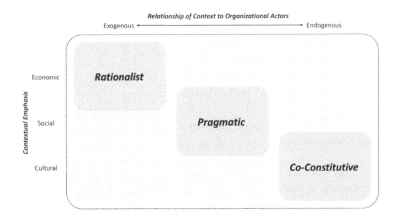

Figure 1.1   Ontology in contemporary organization theory

While each category has a prototypical focus (shaded in dark gray), some theories within these categories extend the range of contextual emphasis (shaded in lighter gray). That is, while rationalist approaches primarily emphasize economic aspects of an organization's context, some rationalist approaches place a greater emphasis on social or cultural aspects of the context. Similarly, some co-constitutive theories might focus on economic or social aspects of context even though most co-constitutive theories emphasize cultural context. Although we focus on elaborating prototypical theories, we briefly acknowledge theoretical examples that stretch our theoretical categories beyond the prototypical focus. These deviations from the prototypes are important, because they highlight the fuzziness and complexity of organization theory as a scholarly field while expanding the range of possibilities for theoretical novelty. Below, we briefly introduce each of our theoretical categories – rationalist, pragmatic, and co-constitutive.

Rationalist theories, such as more economically oriented, managerialist approaches to organizations, focus on organizational decision-making. While an organization's environment is considered exogenous, it is often viewed as a set of economic forces that constrain the nature of decision-making, making some decision choices unviable. As we alluded to above, at the extreme, organizational ecologists conceptualize the environment as so potent and constraining that organizational decision-making provides only the illusion of rationality, as they imagine the outcomes of these choices to be randomly distributed. Nonetheless, rationalist theories tend to employ a rational choice calculus whereby decisions are often explained in terms of optimizing costs versus benefits. While some theories may also try to account for the roles of social relationships and cultural norms, these factors are considered to be exogenous constraints. For example, some structuralist forms of network theory (e.g., Burt, 1982) emphasize the social nature of an organization's context, but view it as exogenous to an organization. Likewise, in areas such as international business, some theories are rooted in a rationalist perspective, conceptualizing context as exogenous to organizations (Hofstede, 1980). Thus, although rationalist theories may conceptualize an organization's environment in different ways, they emphasize the economic aspects of an organization's environment, and generally assume that contextual forces are best understood as exogenous to organizations (e.g., Snidal, 2013).

As we discuss in Chapter 2, rationalist theories are undergirded by utilitarian philosophy. Utilitarianism is a family of moral and political philosophies used to conceptualize general utility or social welfare as the sole ethical value or good to be maximized (e.g., Bentham, 1789; Hume, 1751; Mill, 1863). This philosophy was explicitly leveraged to develop a normative economic approach that embraced a hedonistic version of utilitarianism from the latter part of the 18th century well into the 20th century – that is, a theory of how people, as independent and autonomous actors, should make decisions. This seeded the development of what is referred to as neoclassical economics (i.e., a mathematical approach to the study of supply and demand) by theorizing how production costs relate to consumers' efforts to maximize their utility, such as making purchasing decisions that result in the highest level of satisfaction (Marshall, 1890). While many approaches to strategic management or contingency theories of organization do not explicitly acknowledge linkages to utilitarianism, their focus on decision-making that optimizes or maximizes organizational performance are implicitly grounded in utilitarian philosophy as expressed in rational choice economics.

Pragmatic theories emphasize the social nature of an organization's environment and organizations' practical work to navigate both the constraints and opportunities created by social relationships and processes. Unlike rationalist theories, organizations are not assumed to be independent and autonomous from each other and their context. Instead, the environmental context of organizations tends to be conceptualized as more interpenetrated (partly endogenous and partly exogenous) with organizational actors. We label these theories *pragmatic* following Granovetter (2017), who embraced pragmatist thought in the development of his approach to relational embeddedness (see also Gross, 2009; Tavory & Timmermans, 2013). We believe that this general imagery holds for many other theories that emphasize socio-political dynamics as well – including theories as diverse as resource dependence, the behavioral theory of the firm, and research at the interface of social movements and organizations that emphasize how behavior is influenced by pragmatic or practical-evaluative considerations (Emirbayer & Mische, 1998). While social aspects of the environment tend to be more central for pragmatic theories, some pragmatic scholars also emphasize economic aspects as prominently as they do the social (e.g., resource dependence theorists), while others emphasize the importance of culture alongside economic and social aspects of an organization's context (e.g., Granovetter, 2017). As signaled by the label we have assigned to this ideal-typical class of theories, we consider these approaches to comport with pragmatist philosophy.

Pragmatism originated with late-19th-century American philosophers such as Charles Sanders Peirce, William James, and John Dewey. It is a practical, action-oriented philosophy that considers language and ideas as tools for problem solving and behavior. By focusing on practical action, pragmatists embraced applying the scientific method to understand human behavior, seeking to reform mainstream idealist and realist philosophy that conceptualized human knowledge as something beyond what science could grasp. Contemporary neo-pragmatism builds on the pragmatist tradition by offering a nominalist approach that infers the meanings of words by focusing on how they are used rather than the objects they represent (e.g., Rorty, 1989). Pragmatism is broadly appealing in management, as it offers an important alternative to utilitarian philosophy and rationalist approaches by zooming in on the nature of human actors and the importance of processes such as learning and coping with ambiguity in a pluralistic world. This tradition also undergirds more humanistic approaches in classical management theory, as exemplified by the work of Mary Parker Follet, who emphasized the importance of relationships in the workplace and was an advocate for worker participation and empowerment (see Bednarek & Smith, 2023; Hinings & Meyer, 2018).

Co-constitutive theories conceptualize an organization's environment as endogenous to organizational action, emphasizing the centrality of culture and meaning-making processes. By invoking the notion of co-constitution, we seek to emphasize how wider socio-cultural dynamics constitute organizational identities, and, in turn, how organizational behavior shapes meanings and practices of other actors in the environment. This category includes institutional theory, sensemaking, and practice theory. Although these theories have some overlaps with pragmatic theories, they are more antithetical to rationalist approaches. For instance, we note how some institutional theory scholarship may be undergirded more by pragmatic assumptions than by co-constitutive assumptions. While most co-constitutive theories foundationally emphasize cultural aspects of context, many co-constitutive scholars blend attention to culture with economic and social aspects of context, as exemplified by Callon's (2021) approach to the sociology of markets. Like the other two theoretical categories, there are many important deviations from the core prototypes we emphasize, highlighting the need – and opportunity – for scholars to understand and appreciate the multitude of differences that exist within organization theory.

Philosophically, many co-constitutive theories are sympathetic to phenomenological approaches (e.g., Heidegger, 1962; Husserl, 1970; Merleau-Ponty, 1964) which have inspired much research in organization studies focused on broader socio-cultural developments that profoundly structure conscious experience and the conditions of possibility for intentional action (Meyer, 2008). Phenomenology refers to the philosophical study of the structures of lived experience and consciousness (including judgments, perceptions, and emotions). On this account, "a phenomenon is not a sign or symbol that stands for something else, but rather that which shows itself from itself" (Gehman, 2021a: 241). In this way, phenomenology provides a distinctive starting point from more reductionist philosophies such as utilitarianism that rely on Cartesian analytics to conceptualize the world in terms of objects (e.g., organizations) and how they act and react in relationship to each other. While phenomenology has many variants, it has had a major ontological impact on organization theory as a general philosophical orientation.

In this book, we discuss each of these three ideal-typical categories of theories and their distinctive ontological foundations more extensively. While we focus on particular groupings in the ontological dimensions we feature, this does not necessary exclude the possibility that other ideal-typical theoretical categories exist. For instance, many older sociological approaches to behavior in the mid-20th century Parsonsian tradition might coalesce around an ideal type with a contextual emphasis on culture that is conceptualized as exogenous to organizational actors. In these so-called "oversocialized" approaches to socio-economic life (Wrong, 1961), culture is conceived as an overwhelming structural force that allows for little human or organizational agency outside of what is normatively proscribed. Thus, while theories or theoretical orientations exist outside of our three ideal typical categories of organization theories, and some scholars may object to the particular ways we have grouped their scholarship, we believe there is great value in foregrounding how core ontological assumptions shape organization theorizing.

Regrettably, it is not unusual in our field to see bitter disputes. Sometimes, this happens between scholars who largely share key ontological assumptions, and who might be better served by engaging in constructive dialogue about how to build bridges between theories to potentially generate a broader, more integrative scholarly conversation. Other times, scholars too easily express appreciation for pieces of scholarship that are ontologically oppositional. In these cases, bridges are harder to build – for instance, across rationalist and co-constitutive theories – and a more critical and reflective dialogue about ontology may be more appropriate. Thus, our overall contention is that scholars would be well served by understanding the importance of ontology to organization theorizing, and to engage in mindful ontological reflection as they cultivate their scholarly identities.

1.4   The role of power in organization theory

Power is an important concept in organization theory (Perrow, 1986). It undergirds the structure of society and economy, reinforcing inequality rooted in class and status, as well as authority relationships inside organizations and patterns of behavior in markets and politics. Power is most often conceptualized as a relational phenomenon, rather than as a commodity or resource that actors can possess (Clegg, 1989; Clegg, Courpasson, & Phillips, 2006; Emerson, 1962). In his overview of power in organization theory, Lawrence (2008) highlighted two modes which he labeled "episodic" and "systemic." While episodic power typically involves relatively discrete strategic acts of mobilization initiated by self-interested actors, systemic power often operates through taken-for-granted institutions where rules and routines provide advantages to some actors over others without explicit struggles over the nature of those advantages.

While attention to power dynamics varies dramatically across different organization theories, there have been many complaints over the years, especially from critical management scholars, that attention to power in organization theory has been limited (Munir, 2015; Willmott, 2015). Some have argued that this inattention to power may have grown as organization theory scholars became increasingly affiliated with business schools, focusing on more delimited (and sanitized) managerial problems as opposed to big social problems where there is more of a need to speak truth to power (e.g., Stern & Barley, 1996). While we see signs of this changing as management scholars increasingly seek to focus on grand challenges (Ferraro, Etzion, & Gehman, 2015; Gümüsay et al., 2022) and engaged scholarship (Hoffman, 2021a; Van de Ven, 2007), we also feel that some of the complaints about inattention to power may be a bit overblown.

We believe that the ontological distinctions in organization theory that we focalize have affected the extent to which power is revealed in research. For instance, in rationalist theories, power is rarely dealt with explicitly, aside from some minor references to "market power," primarily found in policy-oriented research in industrial organization economics, where monopolistic and oligopolistic forms of market competition are an analytical focus (e.g., Bain, 1968; Mason, 1957). We believe that many pragmatic and co-constitutive theorists have tried to grapple with power dynamics more explicitly than rationalist theorists, but much more can be done. For instance, in pragmatic theories such as those related to resource dependence and social movements, as well as network theory and the behavioral theory of the firm, episodic power is often attended to in very explicit ways. While power often is less explicitly specified in co-constitutive theories, especially sensemaking and practice theory, Lawrence (2008) highlighted that institutional theory does address episodic and systemic power. While we do not provide a thorough analysis of how power is addressed across organization theory in this book, we encourage early career scholars to critically reflect on how ontological assumptions may shape how power is invoked in both the research they consume as well as the research they produce. Moreover, we urge all scholars to strive towards asking bigger questions in contexts where power dynamics are at play, and to be more explicit about how power shapes the organizational dynamics being studied (Battilana & Casciaro, 2021).

1.5 Ontology, theoretical research communities, and scholarly identity

Ontology is especially important in shaping who we become as scholars. Because ontology has to do with foundational assumptions we make about the world, it shapes how we see the world, as well as the problems we consider and the explanations we develop as scholars. For instance, as we suggested above, utilitarianism guides rationalist theorists towards a focus on how actors make decisions and behave relatively independently from others. Rationalist theorists tend to downplay the importance of social relations and cultural meaning, narrowing the focus to economic forces (e.g., supply and demand) and how they shape organizational decision-making – often aimed at maximizing performance. Thus, when a microeconomic lens is applied to organizations, it can become difficult to see how such decision-making may result in sub-optimal outcomes attributable to pragmatic considerations such as intra-organizational politics or relational interdependencies with other organizations. As a result, theorizing tends to be focused on problems generated by the theoretical conversations to which scholars seek to contribute; likewise, solutions are constructed to appeal to an audience with the same ontological assumptions and orientation.

Of course, this is true of all theories, and each theory tends to have its own audience of scholars who share ontological assumptions and theoretical commitments that foreground their own problems and scholarly answers. Weick (1999) argued that there are often trade-offs regarding three attributes in theory development: generalizability, accuracy, and simplicity (see also McGrath, 1982). These trade-offs may also operate at the level of theoretical research programs undergirded by different ontologies. In the case of microeconomic theory and organizational ecology, for instance, simplicity and generalizability are embraced at the expense of accuracy (e.g., Friedman, 1953). Scholars who are committed to pragmatic and co-constitutive theoretical orientations tend to embrace different mixes of these dimensions in different studies, all of which tend to provide more accuracy than rationalist theories. Hence, while these theories tend to say much less about how decision-making is driven by economic considerations such as supply, demand, and performance maximization, they shed light on different aspects of the world such as the importance of relational interdependence and the interpenetration of organizations and their environment. As a result, they tend to be less simple and elegant. These differences can create conflicts between groups of scholars – for instance, strategy scholars who embrace economics complain that the behavioral theory of the firm (a pragmatic theory) is too complicated to be useful.

It is important to stress that there is a crucial social dimension to the development of scholars and scholarship. As we have been arguing, ontological assumptions become embedded within particular theoretical research communities with specific tastes regarding which problems are important and what kinds of answers (and thus research) are considered adequate – with the right mix of generalizability, accuracy and simplicity. So, to conduct research that others might care about (and cite), one typically needs to join a theoretical research community – to be part of a particular theoretical conversation. For most young scholars, this often happens unwittingly, depending on which Ph.D. program they happen to choose, and within that program, which established scholar is willing to supervise them. These choices, which often occur without a deep understanding of the scholarly field they are entering, provide foundational imprints, since most young scholars tend to be socialized into and develop research agendas that are symbiotic with those of their mentors – at least initially.

It is within these theoretical research communities that scholars develop an understanding of how to conduct research, including an appreciation of which methods and kinds of data are most acceptable, as well as how to craft arguments and evidence in a way that is considered to advance theory – a core criterion for publishing in top tier management journals. As Murray Davis (1971) argued, the most prominent papers in a field are those that are considered interesting – somehow counterintuitive, novel, or otherwise worthy of attention. However, such perceptions and judgments are rendered by specific audiences of other scholars. So, to develop theoretical contributions that are interesting, it is imperative to develop a deep appreciation for how other scholars in one's target audience think.

This often requires getting to know fellow scholars through conferences, meetings and other gatherings well enough to have them comment on work in progress and help cultivate arguments and evidence that they and others like them will find interesting. In a sense, interesting research is co-constructed in ongoing dialogue with other scholars. It is this social grounding of scholarship in theoretical research communities with common research commitments (including ontological assumptions) that, in turn, profoundly shapes the identities and identity positioning of scholars in a field. Most scholars come to be known by the scholarship they produce and the scholars they interact with; thus, many of us come to be known and self-identify as, for instance, transaction cost economists, network analysts, or institutionalists.

However, scholarly identities can also be multiplex. For instance, some scholars in the management subfield of strategy might combine an interest in network theory and analysis with the behavioral theory of the firm and institutional theory. To the extent one is successful in bridging audiences in different theoretical research communities, a scholar's identity might be more robust, and concomitantly attract a larger audience, than a scholar who is more focused on, for instance, network analysis alone. But trying to bridge theoretical conversations with fundamental ontological differences can be more challenging than trying to integrate theories that share ontological assumptions. In the context of our mapping of the organization theory field, we suggest that it is most difficult to bridge rationalist and co-constitutive theories; moreover, whereas pragmatic theories are better suited to be integrated with both rationalist and co-constitutive approaches, efforts to forge connections between pragmatist and co-constitutive theories seem to be more fruitful.

As one drills down further, many potential minefields become apparent. For instance, scholars may take different ontological positions within a category of theories (rationalist, pragmatic, co-constitutive), leading to hostility among those in similar camps. Many examples abound. Conventional microeconomists, for example, have a strong distaste for institutional economists; along with other more recent strands of economics that deviate from pure neoclassical economic assumptions, institutional economics has been branded as heterodox (Foldvary, 1996). While heterodox economic theories are better able to connect to pragmatic organization theories, they retain a strong rationalist flavor, making such integration challenging. Within practice theory, a variety of approaches and scholars embrace different ontological positions within and across pragmatic and co-constitutive theories, creating conflicts, for instance, over approaches to the study of organizational processes (Langley, 1999). Thus, it is important to develop a finer grained appreciation of the nature of particular theoretical conversations and scholars in relation to each other before attempting any bridging efforts.

In our experience, some of the most interesting and impactful scholars have cultivated robust identities and strong ontological positions. A strong ontological position often gives arguments more of an edge, thereby distinguishing them from theoretical conversations that promote other ontological assumptions. While there is a danger of narrowing the audience, it is also possible to cultivate a broader audience by ensuring that research speaks to scholars from other theoretical conversations. While a scholar with a strong ontological position may seek integration across theories, some prominent scholars also seek to engage in debates with scholars from other theoretical camps, highlighting how different theories frame similar phenomena differently (Astley, 1985). Even though there are different strategies for cultivating a robust scholarly identity, the general point is that a more robust identity requires scholars to communicate and interact with a larger, more diverse audience that may or may not share one's ontological assumptions. This includes not just other academics, but also practitioners and wider publics (Hannigan, 2023), whose different ontological lenses implicitly or explicitly shape how they understand and interpret the world. Thus, we believe that understanding the ontological landscape of the field is crucial as one navigates potential opportunities for developing a more robust scholarly identity.

1.6   How the book unfolds

In the next three chapters, we unpack each of the ontological types in organization theory. In Chapter 2, we provide an overview of different rationalist theories that are grounded in utilitarian ideas, and in Chapter 3, we discuss various pragmatic theories that are informed by pragmatist philosophy. In Chapter 4, we review various co-constitutive theoretical approaches that tend to embrace phenomenology. In each chapter, we provide a general overview of different theoretical conversations and highlight key additional readings that may help cultivate a more comprehensive understanding of the organization theory field. Table 1.1 provides an overview of the specific theoretical packages covered by these three chapters.

After unpacking different variants of rationalist, pragmatic, and co-constitutive theories, we shift our attention in Chapter 5 to highlighting the broad reach of organization theory. In particular, we focus on two key domains of scholarship where organization theory and research informed by organization theory has had tremendous influence – entrepreneurship and strategy. These more applied domains of knowledge are particularly relevant because many organization theorists are hired to teach these topics. We discuss how rationalist, pragmatic, and co-constitutive theories play out in the fields of entrepreneurship and strategy to reinforce one of our key arguments about the importance of ontological differences. It is crucial to contemplate not only how these differences affect our research and scholarly identities, but also – insofar as our teaching reflects our research – how these ontological commitments may manifest in the classroom, ultimately shaping how students think about the world.

In Chapter 6, we synthesize insights from the previous chapters, thereby providing a roadmap to help organization scholars build robust scholarly identities and produce novel research contributions that advance the field in impactful ways. Developing such identities imbues organization theorists with the power to meaningfully contribute to multiple academic conversations and maximize the potential for real-world relevance across diverse contexts. We see an opportunity for organization scholars to multiply their potential for impact by developing multivocal and multiplex insights that can speak to multiple audiences (inside and outside

Table 1.1   Overview of theoretical packages

Perspective	Rationalist	Pragmatic	Co-constitutive
Contextual emphasis	Economic	Social	Cultural
Relationship between context and organizational actors	Exogenous	Partially endogenous	Endogenous
Undergirding philosophy	Utilitarianism	Pragmatism	Phenomenology
Example theories	Rational choice Organizational ecology Contingency theory	Behavioral theory of the firm Resource dependence Embeddedness and networks Social movements and organizations	Institutional theory Sensemaking Practice theory

academia) who inhabit diverse thought worlds and embrace a plurality of values positions.

In developing this roadmap, we reprise our key arguments about ontology and emphasize the importance of mindfully engaging with specific audiences and fully understanding their ontological positions. We highlight specific ways organizational scholars can add value and have positive impacts on their institutions, the academy, and the general public. We believe organization theorists with robust scholarly identities are uniquely positioned to be the standard bearers for collegiality in higher education, and thus have great potential to protect and strengthen academic institutions and the foundations of scholarship. Beyond the walls of academic institutions, robust identities provide scholars with a platform for engaging with diverse stakeholders in the public square. Rather than offering narrow prescriptions, organization scholars are uniquely positioned to foster theoretically informed understandings about how particular lines of action produce particular consequences. Such an approach is especially useful in the context of grand challenges, which we encourage organization scholars to study. We conclude the book by considering the burgeoning research on grand challenges through the lens of our framework of ontological differences and the quest for a robust identity. This illustration reveals exciting possibilities for organization scholars to bridge different literatures and establish links between different communities.

Notes

1   What Burrell and Morgan (1979) called nominalism, others have called idealism (DeLanda, 2009; Snape & Spencer, 2003). A third ontological position, materialism, is a variant of realism (DeLanda, 2009; Snape & Spencer, 2003).

2. Rationalist theories

Rationalist theories orient scholarship to the importance of material resources to organizational decision-making, performance, and survival. They include rational choice theory, evolutionary perspectives such as organizational ecology, and contingency theories. As exemplified by rational choice approaches such as neoclassical economics, rationalist theories share distinctive ontological and axiological assumptions that have roots in utilitarian philosophy (Driver, 2022; Rawls, 1993). Relative to the framework we introduced in the previous chapter, these theories tend to assume that there is an objective reality independent of perceptions that consequentially shapes organizational outcomes.

With regard to contextual orientation, rationalist theories embrace economic explanations for action and presume that an organization's environment is exogenous. This is because they start with a world in which actors are "born pre-equipped to act through essential inherent causal mechanisms (reasons as causes) that drive action on their own autonomous momentum" (Somers, 1998: 764). For instance, a core ontological assumption of rational choice theory is that "action is purposive, intentional, and involves means-ends calculations" (Kiser & Hechter, 1998: 798). In addition, most rationalist theories assume self-interest with the goal of wealth maximization (Kiser & Hechter, 1998; Somers, 1998). These assumptions are stronger than "just a commitment to individualism"; they encompass "a causal ontology in which agential intentionality is posited to be the a priori causal force/mechanism at work in the social world" (Somers, 1998: 750). While these theories vary in the extent of choice an actor has, they universally emphasize the material resource dynamics associated with an organization's environment. We discuss various kinds of rationalist theories and elaborate on their utilitarian foundations below.

2.1   Philosophical foundations of rationalist theories: utilitarianism

At their core, rationalist theories embrace a functionalist paradigm; that is, they take a realist, positivist, deterministic, and nomothetic approach that seeks "to provide essentially rational explanations of social affairs" (Burrell & Morgan, 1979: 26). To do so, they deploy biological or mechanical analogies as a means of modeling and explaining social phenomena. As part of this overall orientation, rationalist theories aspire to be instrumentally useful, for instance, by prescribing managerial best practices (Reinecke, Boxenbaum, & Gehman, 2022). They are also committed to a particular normative or axiological code. Namely, they presume a competitive, calculative, and market driven logic that espouses utility or welfare maximization as the highest ideal. Accordingly, we view utilitarianism as providing the philosophical foundations that undergird the package of ontological commitments of rationalist theories.

The development of utilitarianism can be traced to 18th- and 19th-century philosophers and economists such as Jeremy Bentham, David Hume, John Stuart Mill, Henry Sidgwick, and Adam Smith (Driver, 2022; Rawls, 1993). "The key idea was that people should be thought of as consumers in relation to government policy and that the aim of such policy should be to maximize overall consumer satisfaction" (Pettit, 2005: 158). From a utilitarianism perspective, society is understood in terms of political solidarism; people are conceived as unified agents bound together by a singular set of beliefs, desires, values and so forth. To wit, the maximization criterion is typically assessed by simply adding up individual welfares or utilities to arrive at overall consequences (Sen & Williams, 1982), thereby moving from individual well-being to collective well-being. Although initially these ideas were political, eventually they were taken up by economists who advocated for utilitarian measures of public welfare as well as techniques such as cost-benefit analysis. It follows from such assumptions that "rational" behavior is that which is utilitarian.

Utilitarianism also pervades many approaches to grand challenges, a theme we revisit in greater depth later in the book. Take, for instance, the concept of "ecosystem services." Mainstream approaches typically value such services instrumentally, that is, in terms of their capacity to satisfy human preferences.

> The overall value of utility provided by a piece of woodland in the form of carbon sequestration, recreational opportunities and beauty can be quantified, and then compared to the value of food or biofuels from an alternative agricultural land use. This allows decision makers to choose the land use generating the greatest overall utility to society. (Craig et al., 2019: 813)

Environmental degradation is similarly conceived as an information problem, one that can be corrected by injecting signals (e.g., market prices, taxes) that seek to ameliorate sub-optimal choices – importantly, by appealing to utilitarian motives.

Evident here is utilitarianism's embrace of a specific conception of morality, or what we call an axiological code. At the center of this code is the pursuit of self-interest and an insatiable desire for consumption. Such appropriation is "seen not only as rational, but also as morally right, since the maximization of individual utility is conceived [as], and the guiding principle of … social order" (Muradian & Gómez-Baggethun, 2021: 6). From within this axiology, self-restraint is seen as rational only to the extent that it pays off later, and even then, only to the extent that it clears the relevant net present value hurdles.

Utilitarianism is most explicitly evident in rational choice theories, but has consequently shaped most rationalist theories. According to Reus-Smith, rationalist theories hew to four primary assumptions. First, rationalists are individualists; "they treat individual human actors as the irreducible units of analysis" (Reus-Smit, 2018: 158). Second, individuals have coherent preferences which they pursue strategically. Importantly, rational action contrasts starkly from action driven by social norms, in which individuals engage in practices for their own sake, not for their consequences. Third, the pursuit of one's preferences is subject to environmental constraints. Fourth, individuals are rational in their pursuits. As Elster (2001: 12767) put it: "Rational choice theory is consequentialist, in that it enjoins people to act in certain ways because of the expected outcomes." In other words, rationalist theories are at once positive and normative. Rational choice theories tell agents what they must do to achieve their ends as efficiently as possible (Elster, 2001). This augers back to Max Weber's (1978) famous concept of instrumentally rational action (*zweckrational*), wherein actions are pursued only after evaluating their consequences and considering various means of achieving them. In short, "rational choice began as a normative enterprise (Stein, 1999) and lends itself readily to normative analysis, at least along the utilitarian lines from which it developed" (Snidal, 2013: 102).

2.2   Rational choice theories

Rational choice theories are rooted in assumptions underpinning neo-classical economics – a metatheory that focuses on supply and demand as key exogenous forces behind the production, pricing, and consumption of goods and services. From this perspective, actors are assumed to be highly rational decision-makers. Rationality is construed very narrowly as decisions that maximize utility for consumers or maximize profits for organizations. Rational decision-making depends on full information about one's environment (e.g., supply and demand), clear decision-making preferences (e.g., maximization of profit), and the ability to select the best course of action from a given set of alternatives (such as how much of a given product an organization should produce). Thus, decision-making is results-driven.

In addition, competition is valorized over collaboration, which Smith (1976) suggested easily slides into conspiracy. Since the early moments of economic theorizing, it was assumed that competition leads to an efficient allocation of resources within an economy. Most research in conventional microeconomics does not examine what actors actually do, but relies on predictive models that assume all actors behave rationally and competitively.

Neoclassical economics is a prototypical rationalist theory because it assumes that there is always only one best decision to make. Thus, decision-makers might as well be lightning quick calculators (Arrow, 1983); there is no need to consider how decision-makers might be affected by environmental uncertainty, psychological biases, emotions, or alternative forms of rationality. This narrow form of hyper-rationality reminds one of "the old joke about the assistant professor who, when walking with a full professor, reaches down for the $100 bill he sees on the sidewalk. But he is held back by his senior colleague, who points out that if the $100 bill were real, it would have been picked up already" (Olson,

1996: 3). While most economists acknowledge that real-world human decision-makers may not behave exactly as depicted by neoclassical economics, they still defend the parsimonious elegance of their models by arguing that it doesn't matter if actual behavior deviates from their models as long as the models retain their predictive power. In such cases, defenders of rational choice approaches maintain that in the aggregate, actors behave as if they are rational.

And while there may be some truth to these claims, economic models do not always hold up – especially in times of turbulence. For instance, in the wake of the 2008 subprime mortgage meltdown and concomitant global financial collapse, U.S. Federal Reserve Chairman Alan Greenspan admitted that he had failed to recognize a "flaw in the model that I perceived is the critical functioning structure that defines how the world works" (PBS NewsHour, 2008). In fact, some might argue that economic models may even be the drivers of such crises. That is, in many cases, economic models may not depict how markets work, but in a sense provide a normative ideal of how they should work – what Callon (1998a) referred to as performativity. For instance, in the context of the financial derivatives market, MacKenzie and Millo (2003: 107) showed that models related to "option pricing theory – a 'crown jewel' of neoclassical economics – succeeded empirically not because it discovered preexisting price patterns but because markets changed in ways that made its assumptions more accurate and because the theory was used in arbitrage."

Nonetheless, rational choice theories rooted in economics are powerfully seductive and tend to be an effective rhetorical tool in policy circles, despite their empirical failings. Many economists and scholars in political science and sociology who embrace rational choice have, over the years, tried to amend the core neoclassical economic theory to better account for its blind spots and shortfalls. For instance, institutional economists, while retaining assumptions of rationality and competition, have sought to better account for processes related to organizational and institutional change that are bracketed by the neoclassical economic tradition. An important strand of institutional economics focuses on transactions – or what some refer to as transaction cost economics (e.g., Williamson, 1975, 1985).

Building on Coase (1937), Oliver Williamson (1981) sought to develop theory about the make (produce in-house) versus buy (contract with other organizations) decision – that is, the conditions under which production activities are organized within a firm or through the market. While this decision is assumed to be driven by a cost calculus where managers should choose the lower cost option (that is, the one that is most efficient), Williamson deviated from narrow assumptions of rationality found in neoclassical economics, instead adopting the idea of bounded rationality put forth by Herbert Simon (1957). The notion of bounded rationality aims to capture how human decision-making departs from perfect economic rationality due to limited cognitive capacity, as well as information and time constraints.

Simon, his colleague Jim March, and others associated with the Carnegie School (discussed in the next chapter) emphasized how bounded rationality often leads to suboptimal decisions, or what they referred to as satisficing. In contrast, Williamson invoked bounded rationality more as a way to explain deviations from rationality without unpacking in more detail how make versus buy decisions were made. For instance, Williamson was quite vague on how to actually measure transaction costs. However, his theory suggests that with a high level of bounded rationality and asset specificity in a given contract relationship, the transaction costs of using the market increase, making it more likely that a firm will pursue vertical integration. Collaboration is difficult to imagine in Williamson's (1975: 255) framework because it assumes there is always the possibility that a firm's partner will be opportunistic – defined as "self-interest seeking with guile;" being risk averse, we act accordingly.

Williamson's pioneering work has been very influential and has provided one of the most prominent foundations for the development of economic approaches to organizations over the past half-century. However, this line of research remains committed to rational choice under constraints, whether in the form of cognitive limits on information processing or exogenous environmental constraints associated with demand, supply, or opportunism. Organizational economists, like economists more generally, have tried to increasingly account for dynamics such as collaboration, trust, and generosity, which seem to contradict assumptions such as opportunism and a focus on cost calculation.

They have done this by developing an expanded notion of self-interest (or utility). For instance, Leibenstein (1966) developed the idea of X-efficiency to account for the divergence of a firm's observed behavior in practice from the efficient behavior assumed or implied by neoclassical economic theory. This line of thinking gave rise to an important new subfield of behavioral economics that, building on Simon's pioneering work, combined elements of economics and psychology to understand how and why people behave the way they do in the real world (Kahneman & Tversky, 1979). Thus, behavioral economics fundamentally differs from neoclassical economics, which assumes that most people have static, well-defined, exogenously defined preferences and make well-informed, self-interested decisions based on those preferences.

Over time, this notion has enabled economists to incorporate various explanatory factors, including morality, into definitions of self-interest to account for deviations from the canonical theory. Gary Becker (1976) leveraged this sensibility to expand the economics discipline beyond the economic realm to account for processes such as discrimination and general human behavior in the family, other social realms, and even human happiness (Thaler & Sunstein, 2008). This has enabled the economics discipline to become even more hegemonic, but one has to wonder how far the notion of self-interest can be expanded without losing all value as a concept. Moreover, concerns as diverse as politics, social relations, trust, and culture are substantively ignored. When researching these kinds of topics, it might be more appropriate to draw on theories from other categories discussed in the next two chapters that embrace quite different ontological assumptions.

2.3   Organizational ecology

Organizational ecology is a theory seeded by the pioneering work of Hannan and Freeman (1977), who sought to answer the question of why there are so many different kinds of organizations. While distinctive from rational choice theories in economics, the theory they developed with colleagues over the years (see Carroll & Hannan, 2000 for a summary) had a more economic bent to it through its emphasis on competition over material resources as a driving factor. In contrast to the economic focus on rational choice, organizational ecology has been criticized mainly for its bracketing of choice in favor of a theory of organizations that was more environmentally deterministic – driven by consumer demand (Astley & Van de Ven, 1983).

In brief, organizational ecology posited that organizations compete for resources in niche spaces, however their goal is not profit maximization, but survival. Organizational ecologists advanced a pessimistic view on what organizations could actually do to enhance their chances of survival. They asserted that most organizations ultimately fail, and that efforts to transform a failing organization into one that is more suited to a shifting environment have a very low probability of success. Thus, survival of any particular organization, like any particular animal in a herd, is considered to be random.

Organizational ecologists developed an analytical strategy that involved developing life histories of populations of organizations. Given that populations became their focal unit of analysis, organizational ecology was often referred to as population ecology. The empirical research program documented, across many life histories of organizational populations (e.g., automobile manufacturers, newspapers, labor unions), a common pattern of slow initial growth (which included a high organizational failure rate), followed by a dramatic rise of the number of organizations in a population with a much lower rate of failure. They argued that this pattern reflected the difficulty of attracting consumers to a new population of entrepreneurial organizations, but that as a population gained legitimacy, new organizations would be created and all organizations would more or less thrive. Organizational ecologists were often criticized for failing to measure legitimacy independent of organizational density, and more generally neglecting the role of cultural processes (e.g., Baum & Powell, 1995; Zucker, 1989).

Organizational ecologists documented that after an organizational population establishes legitimacy and begins to grow, limits of growth are eventually reached and the population enters a phase of demise, ultimately resulting in extinction. Supposedly driven by a population hitting its resource carrying capacity limit, the organizational failure rate begins to increase and accelerate as consumers shift their attention to other kinds of organizational products and services. Again, organizational ecologists paid very little attention to how and why individual organizations failed or consumer demand waned, focusing instead on parsimoniously arguing that decreased density of an organizational population must be driven by a decline in resources, and thus, a reduction in the legitimacy of a particular organizational form.

Organization ecology was considered a very prominent and important paradigm in the 1980s and 1990s, prompting Pfeffer (1993) to proclaim that the organizational ecology paradigm was a model for what all organization theories should become. While his argument was rooted in a concern for how the field of organization theory, like a niche space for any organizational population, might be in decline in the face of competition from the powerful discipline of economics, Pfeffer was publicly rebuked by others who rejected both his characterization of the organization theory field, as well as his proposed solution (e.g., Van Maanen, 1995).

Ironically, it is not the field of organization theory that has been diminished over time, but the paradigm of organizational ecology, which has become somewhat of a niche area. Whether this is driven more by waning scholarly interest in the rise and fall of organizational populations, or the fact that the paradigm has failed to provide a sufficient backbone for a more general theory that could be as expansive as rational choice economics is unclear. However, it does provide a good example of how prominent approaches (or conversations) in organization theory may not remain so. From a sociology of knowledge perspective, organization theory has no master theory, but instead embraces a plurality of perspectives. This is due, at least in part, to the fact that the study of organizations and organizing is a complex terrain requiring a multitude of vantage points.

Beyond organizational ecology exists a broader set of more synthetic and cosmopolitan evolutionary perspectives on organizations that are much less tethered to rational choice theory and embrace a variety of ideas found in pragmatic and co-constitutive theories (e.g., Aldrich, 1979; Aldrich, Ruef, & Lippmann, 2020; Baum & Singh, 1994). While these approaches often provide useful meta-theories rooted in biological ideas that can enable generative integration across theories, evolutionary scholars tend to downplay (or ignore) the kinds of ontological distinctions we foreground in this book. As a result, early career scholars interested in employing evolutionary frameworks risk using concepts in superficial ways and invoking concepts from multiple theoretical conversations that do not easily mesh. As long as ontological concerns are mindfully considered, we believe that evolutionary approaches provide a potentially fruitful avenue for more integrative research, although they have not yet matured into a growing theoretical conversation on their own.

2.4   Contingency theory

Contingency theory represents a departure from rational choice economics and organizational ecology, but still fits best in the rationalist category of theories. Contingency theory arguably represents some of the most applied management theories. As noted in Chapter 1, these theories emphasize how economic conditions and external pressures create constraints that trigger managerial changes in organizational design to improve performance or ensure organizational survival. Thus, contingency theory leverages various kinds of practice-oriented administrative theories to identify optimal organizational designs for different environmental conditions (e.g., Burns & Stalker, 1961; Lawrence & Lorsch, 1967; Thompson, 1967). Whereas earlier administrative theories sought to develop universal prescriptions for how to optimally organize a firm, contingency theorists argued that there was not one best way to organize.

Hinings and Meyer (2018: 51) noted that contingency theorists developed a comparative approach to organizations "in order to study both similarities and differences among them. The emphasis became one of contextualizing and explaining similarities and differences, suggesting that there are multiple types of organizations and multiple best ways." But like earlier administrative theories, organizations still tended to be conceptualized as rational tools that managers can manipulate to achieve goals – typically, enhanced performance.

These theories mainly conceptualize an organization's environment as comprising an exogenous set of material resources, and posit that different kinds of organizational designs are required depending on different levels and kinds of environmental uncertainty (Milliken, 1987). James D. Thompson's (1967) book, *Organizations in Action*, a landmark contribution to contingency theory, highlighted that "uncertainty appears as the fundamental problem for complex organizations, and coping with uncertainty, as the essence of the administrative process" (p. 159). Thompson conceptualized organizations as complex open systems whose appropriate structures and systems were "indeterminate and faced with uncertainty, but at the same time as subject to criteria of rationality and hence needing determinateness and certainty" (p. 10).

Foreshadowing March's (1991) famous emphasis on the need for organizations to balance exploration and exploitation, Thompson (1967) went on to suggest that a fundamental paradox of administration revolves around the dual search for both certainty and flexibility. He then detailed different types of uncertainty and how organizational designs might shift depending on different sources of environmental uncertainty, with each organizational design aiming to protect (or buffer) the technical core of an organization. At around the same time, Lawrence and Lorsch (1967), often credited for coining the term "contingency theory," emphasized how different levels of uncertainty create problems for different aspects of an organization, necessitating different degrees and forms of integration or differentiation among and across organizational subunits.

In focusing on the variety of ways organizations may be restructured in response to environmental conditions, this research contributed to a much richer comparative analysis of organizations and organizing. For instance, Woodward (1965) highlighted how links between different kinds of technology and production systems (small scale, large scale, or continuous process) necessitated different kinds of organizational structures to be effective. The Aston Group also conducted a series of comparative organizational studies that unpacked the relationship between organizational structure and context (e.g., Pugh, Hickson, & Hinings, 1969; Pugh et al., 1969; Pugh, Hickson, Hinings, & Turner, 1968; for reviews, see Donaldson & Luo, 2014; Pugh & Hickson, 2007). This led to the creation of various kinds of typological theories of organizing (e.g., Blau & Scott, 1962; Burns & Stalker, 1961; Etzioni, 1961). While contingency theory is not a vibrant area of research today, its insights continue to permeate contemporary theoretical conversations, as well as management teaching.

2.5   Discussion

In this chapter, we have provided an overview of three rationalist organization theories – rational choice theory, organizational ecology, and contingency theory. We have argued that these theories share ontological commitments undergirded by utilitarian philosophy. This includes a valorization of the economic sphere, a focus on individual or organizational self-interest and instrumental action, and the treatment of organizational environments as exogenous. Although these ontological commitments are most explicit in rational choice theories as exemplified by neoclassical economics and other economic approaches to organizational behavior, they are evident across rationalist organization theories more generally.

For instance, contingency theory's core proposition is that organizational viability depends on the extent to which an organization fits with its environment. It is hard to miss the Darwinian and functionalist "biology" at work here. Indeed, consistent with this "organismic analogy," an organization's chances of survival depend on achieving an appropriate match between its internal structure and the demands imposed by its tasks, environment, and members (Burrell & Morgan, 1979: 164). In turn, differentiation, integration, and adaptation are central concerns, but variably so, depending on the munificence and dynamism of the environment. Teleologically speaking, organizations "need" to survive; this need, which has been likened to a "functional imperative" (p. 168), equips them with purposive rationality in relation to the economic system. Interestingly, this need has rhetorical value as well (Sillince, 2005).

Organizational ecology shares contingency theory's concern with adaptation and survival, but challenges the extent to which managers or organizations are likely to succeed in making such adjustments. For organizational ecologists, if adaptation is to occur, it is more likely to be found at the population level, for instance, from newly entering organizations. More generally, vital rates (i.e., births, deaths) in one population of organizations can have fateful consequences for those of another, functionally impacting organizations through adaptation or selection. As a result, "the theory and methods of organizational ecology combine to make it a case of positivism in one of its strongest forms in organization studies" (Donaldson, 2005: 48).

An important argument of this book is that different ontological positions offer not only advantages, but also blind spots and related problems. For instance, while neoclassical and fellow rational choice economists seek (and often claim) to provide comprehensive general theories, this is an impossibility in our view. In fact, we find it to be very dangerous to the extent it involves a hegemonic effort to diminish or eradicate rival perspectives and theories that enhance our understanding of the world in a different way. Rationalist theories do have advantages in providing parsimonious approaches to understanding organizational processes, although contingency theory is much less parsimonious than economics or organizational ecology. Nevertheless, the blind spots associated with rationalist theories are numerous.

By conceptualizing an organization's environment as exogenous and primarily consisting of material resources, rationalist theories tend to ignore or downplay the role of social relationships and cultural processes, as well as how organizational behavior is fundamentally intertwined with the behavior of various other actors. Thus, rationalist parsimony comes at the expense of highly de-contextualized theory that ignores important questions and issues related to power. For example: How is rationality inflected and shaped by various interactions and beliefs? To what extent is organizational behavior *not* goal-directed or functionally driven by outcomes such as efficiency and performance? In fact, many scholars who are committed to more pragmatic or co-constitutive ontologies find the rationalist ontology to be impoverished. In the next chapter, we provide an overview of pragmatist theories that foreground the social dynamics of an organization's context, and conceptualize that context as more inter-penetrated with the focal organizations being analyzed.

3. Pragmatic theories

Whereas rationalist theories focus on the importance of material resources to organizational decision-making, performance and survival, pragmatic theories emphasize social relationships and situated dynamics. Economic or cultural aspects of an organization's context are not ignored in pragmatic theories, but they are not the primary focus for organizational action. Ontologically, pragmatic theories draw directly on pragmatism, a uniquely American philosophical tradition that focuses on practical action. At its core, pragmatism seeks "to overcome the Cartesian dualisms" (Joas, 1993: 18; see also Lorino, 2018), such as the assumption that subjects and objects are independent and predetermined, seeing them instead as interdependent and dynamically interrelated (Ansell, 2009; Joas, 1996). The result is "an understanding of intentionality and sociality that differ[s] radically from that of utilitarianism" (Joas, 1993: 18). Although the allure of this tradition waned in the post-World War II era, it has undergone a significant revival in recent decades in philosophy (Rorty, 1979, 1982; for a review, see Gross, 2003), sociology (Ansell, 2011; Gross et al., 2022; Joas, 1993), and organization theory (Farjoun et al., 2015; Lorino, 2018; Parmar et al., 2016).

With regard to contextual orientation, instead of conceptualizing an organization's environment as exogenous, as Granovetter (1985) emphasized, pragmatic theories assume that organizations are socially embedded and that the environment is largely of their own making (Weick, 1979, 2003). These environments are often assumed to be pluralistic, and behavior is often understood as driven by pragmatic or practical evaluative considerations (Emirbayer & Mische, 1998; Kraatz & Block, 2008). This is a consequence of the fact that pragmatist theories depart from traditional understandings of stimulus and response. Instead, "it is action that determines which stimuli are relevant within the context defined by the action" (Joas, 1993: 21). Below, we discuss several broad theoretical conversations, that, while distinctive, share a more pragmatic ontology relative to other organization theories. These include the behavioral theory of the firm, resource dependence, embeddedness, and social movements and organizations.

3.1   Philosophical foundations of pragmatist theories: American pragmatism

Pragmatism offers "a critique of utilitarianism" (Joas, 1993: 59; see also Gross, 2009; Whitford, 2002). In place of self-interest and guile, actors are conceived as "embedded in praxis and sociality prior to any form of conscious intentionality of action;" pragmatism thus "undermines the conception of the individual who calculates in terms of utility at the level of a theory of action" (Joas, 1993: 59–60). In place of utility maximization, pragmatism views problem-solving as the focal activity and emphasizes the "situation" as the relevant unit of analysis (Dewey, 1933; Ferraro et al., 2015; Whitford, 2002). Although problems may sometimes involve utility considerations, pragmatists also are interested in problems as diverse as health, meaning, purpose, and by extension, contemporary themes such as democracy and sustainability (Ansell, 2011).

Pragmatism originated in the United States in the 1870s (Legg & Hookway, 2021). Over the past 150 years, it has emerged as a third major philosophical tradition, alongside analytic and continental approaches. Influential early pragmatists included Charles Sanders Peirce, William James, George Herbert Mead, and John Dewey. Since the 1970s, there has been a resurgence of interest in pragmatism, or what has come to be called neopragmatism, a development traced to Rorty's rebuke of representationalism (Gross, 2003; Rorty, 1979, 1982; Legg & Hookway, 2021). Other notable contributions in recent decades have been made by scholars such as Putnam and Brandom. Although pragmatism is not a unified school of thought, and each of these authors emphasized different topics, a key touchstone is opposition to the Cartesian model of cognition (Legg & Hookway, 2021). Namely, pragmatists seek to circumvent "the dualisms between perceiving and comprehending, facts and values, body and mind, individual and society which arise from the Cartesian approach" (Joas, 1993: 61).

Given its focus on problem-solving, pragmatism resonates with scholars looking to advance our understanding of grand challenges (Ferraro et al., 2015; Gehman et al., 2022). For instance, Ansell (2011) posited that sustainable development serves as a "meta-concept," one that operates as a boundary object, "adaptable to different viewpoints and robust enough to maintain identity across them" (Star & Griesemer, 1989: 387), and thereby multivocal, defying easy definition. These two qualities are generative in his view. As a boundary object, sustainable development has sparked engagement by diverse actors in their quest for possible solutions. Meanwhile, the multivocality of sustainable development has produced ambiguity that is fruitful. Overall, the concept of sustainable development:

> has promoted institution-building activity at every scale of government as well as in the private sector. In addition, it has successfully created processes for reflecting on existing practices, deliberating about alternative futures, and initiating widespread experimentation and innovation. (Ansell, 2011: 60)

In terms of its axiological commitments, pragmatism foregrounds the normativity of all action. Notably, it sees utilitarianism as missing the extent to which normativity underlies action and is even inherent in action itself (Chia & Rasche, 2010; Gehman et al., 2013; MacIntyre, 1981). "Knowing is normative," not in the sense of prescribing how we should conduct ourselves a priori, but rather "how we can act to improve the current situation" (Simpson & den Hond, 2022: 133). At the same time, contrary to functionalist explanations, pragmatists are skeptical of assumptions about teleological tendencies in social systems, such as the preexistence of taken-for-granted values against which action might be rationally aimed or analyzed. Additionally, pragmatists have no problem asking about the normative usefulness of particular research findings. "This criterion allows the pragmatist to make judgments about research where the positivist and antipositivist could not" (Wicks & Freeman, 1998: 130).

Relative to the aims of this book, pragmatism differs from utilitarian philosophy in several ways (Gross, 2009; Whitford, 2002). First, pragmatism centers on problem-solving. Within the domain of organization theory, it is especially well-suited to investigating problems such as organizational change and complexity, as well as problems of administration and industry (Ansell, 2009; Farjoun et al., 2015; Simpson & den Hond, 2022). Second, pragmatists "insist problem situations are always interpreted through cultural lenses" (Gross, 2009: 367). This means that action is context-dependent, taking place within cultural and institutional arrangements that enable and constrain what is thinkable and desirable (e.g., Green et al., 2009; Swidler, 1986). Third, in place of rational calculation and purposive action, pragmatists emphasize habit and practical action, in which there is little conscious weighing of means and ends. Fourth, to the extent that instrumental rationality occurs, it can be understood as a kind of habit. In essence, actors learn how to behave, for instance, as homo economicus, not because doing so is natural or rational per se, but because it is a historically situated and deployed habit (see also Joas, 1993: 196–197). Finally, in contrast with utilitarianism, means and ends are not pregiven, but emerge through action. In this process, actors can come to "see themselves in new ways, to value different kinds of goods, and to become attached to problem solutions they could not have imagined previously" (Gross, 2009: 367).

3.2   Behavioral theory of the firm

The behavioral theory of the firm emerged from what is known as the Carnegie School – a series of scholarly efforts and collaborations initiated by Nobel Prize-winning economist Herbert A. Simon (whose Ph.D. was actually in political science), economist Richard M. Cyert, and political scientist James G. March – who shared an interest in developing more pragmatic approaches to organizations, a topic that was essentially ignored in the neoclassical economics literature. While key work in the early development of this tradition focused mostly on the internal dynamics of organizing and organizational decision-making, over time, scholars have broadened the approach to consider how organizational processes unfold in interaction with broader social dynamics involving actors in an organization's environment.

This tradition was seeded by an important foundational book, *Administrative Behavior* (Simon, 1947), which emphasized the behavioral and cognitive processes that shape decision-making processes. In contrast to rationalist approaches to decision-making, Simon argued that having full knowledge of all alternatives, as well as all consequences that follow from each alternative, is impossible in most situations. Thus, in contrast to homo economicus, decision-makers operate with *bounded rationality* – cognitive limits to knowledge, time, and capacity that prohibit the kind of rational decision-making that is assumed in neoclassical economics. As a result, decision-makers are unable to maximize utility, but make the best decisions they can, given their cognitive limits – what he referred to as *satisficing*. This beachhead statement, stemming from Simon's Ph.D. thesis, catalyzed an effort to develop an approach underpinned by the psychology of intendedly rational agents, thereby undermining core assumptions of conventional rational actor models.

Building on these ideas, a major Carnegie School collaboration between March and Simon resulted in the book *Organizations* (March & Simon, 1958). Often credited as a turning point in the rise of organization studies as a field, they elaborated on Simon's earlier work by embracing cutting edge ideas in cognition at the time. For instance, they highlighted how bounded rationality was animated by cognitive frameworks that created and maintained simplified subjective representations of reality that shaped decision-making. Setting out to develop a more realistic theorization of organizations than extant administrative theories in that era, they conceptualized organizations as coordinative systems that are subject to intra-organizational conflict. Emphasizing that the interrelationship between motivation and cognitive factors must be a central concern for organization theory, they developed a rich array of hypotheses aimed at unpacking the motivations of individuals in an organization, as well as the role of bounded rationality, satisficing, and many other factors that shape organizational decision-making.

In 1963, Cyert and March published *A Behavioral Theory of the Firm*, which extended prior efforts by developing a much more political approach to organizational decision-making, conceptualizing the firm as a coalition of groups (e.g., managers, shareholders, workers, suppliers) where conflict is endemic. In addition, the book lays out a treasure trove of organizational processes related to learning, performance feedback, cognition, attention, goal formation, aspiration levels, resource allocation, and the like, which have become core focal points for scholarship to the present day. Their agenda-setting book emphasized four relational concepts that were at the core of their theorization: quasi-resolution of conflict, uncertainty avoidance, problemistic search, and organizational learning.

The influence of the behavioral theory of the firm has only grown over time, influencing many empirical studies, simulation modeling, and research on cognition and firm strategy. In their review of this research tradition, Gavetti et al. (2012: 2) noted: "*A Behavioral Theory of the Firm* has been extraordinarily influential. Its foundational concepts, assumptions, and aspirations have inspired – and continue to inspire – a vibrant community of behaviorally oriented students of organizations and strategy." Research has continued to blossom on topics central to the behavioral theory of the firm, including the dynamics of routines (Feldman & Pentland, 2003; Nelson & Winter, 1982; Ocasio, 1999), learning (Lant & Mezias, 1992; March, 1991; Miner & Mezias, 1996), attention (Jacobides, 2007; Ocasio, 1997; Rerup, 2009: 200), capabilities (Dosi et al., 2000; Gavetti & Levinthal, 2004; Nelson & Winter, 2002), power (Eisenhardt & Bourgeois, 1988; Hambrick & Mason, 1984; Kaplan, 2008; Ocasio, 1994), search (Gavetti & Levinthal, 2000), and performance feedback (Greve, 1998, 2003). While a good deal of this literature continues to emphasize decision-making processes within organizations, since the foundational Carnegie School statements, most of these works have embraced open systems perspectives where decision-making is understood as influenced by how the organization is interpenetrated with its environment.

This shift to open systems was at least partially influenced by the shift of the Carnegie School from Pennsylvania to California – specifically, Stanford (where March moved to in 1970) – where open systems perspectives such as institutional theory (discussed in the next chapter) were being incubated and developed (Beckman, 2021). Importantly, for the field of organization theory, Carnegie School ideas were so foundational and supple that integrative efforts naturally developed across theoretical conversations such as the behavioral theory of the firm and institutional theory. For instance, a number of studies have examined how organizational attention and decision-making have been reshaped by institutional dynamics. Thornton and Ocasio (1999) and Thornton (2004) examined how changes in an institutional logic (i.e., from an editorial to a market logic) shifted the nature of organizational attention and the determinants of executive succession and strategic decision-making in higher education publishing firms. Lounsbury (2007) built on these studies to show how different institutional logics differentially directed attention and strategic decision-making by mutual fund managers in Boston and New York.

Audia and Greve (2021) highlighted how a more focused theory of performance feedback has expanded the scope of the behavioral theory of the firm in recent years, suggesting further opportunities for integration with institutional theory. While Cyert and March (1963) asserted that problemistic search and subsequent organizational change are triggered when performance dips below an aspiration level, contemporary research on performance feedback has begun to unpack where aspiration levels come from, the dimensions of performance managers attend to and how they react to deviations in performance, as well as how organizations engage in problemistic search and implement organizational change in response to performance feedback. They noted that several novel theoretical developments have emerged due to empirical anomalies such as the fact that firms are often less responsive to performance below original aspiration levels. They suggested that institutional logics shape the variety and can exacerbate the number of goals to which decision-makers must attend, highlighting that a more complete understanding of the dynamics of performance feedback requires attention to how the organization is interpenetrated with its environment. To wit, they called for more research at the interface of the institutional logics perspective (Thornton et al., 2012), which we discuss in the next chapter on co-constitutive theories, and the behavioral theory of the firm.

Research on organizational learning also has developed more social and institutional components – highlighting, for instance, how decision-making is influenced by learning from external sources such as the experiences of other organizations (Levitt & March, 1988). Other work related to both learning and search behavior has emphasized the importance of networks (discussed later in this chapter), showing, for instance, that organizations benefit from greater diversity of network ties to external actors (e.g., Baum et al., 2000; Beckman & Haunschild, 2002; Ingram & Baum, 1997). While this broadening of the behavioral theory of the firm to appreciate the open system nature of organizations has been fruitful, many open questions remain, and more research is required to understand how interorganizational relationships, as well as other field-level actors and beliefs shape and are shaped by the strategic decision-making emphasized in the Carnegie School tradition (Gavetti et al., 2012). Thus, it remains a vibrant area of research at the center of organization theory that robustly connects to a variety of other theories.

3.3   Resource dependence

Resource dependence theory (Pfeffer & Salancik, 1978) is a key organization theory that emphasizes how organizations are in ongoing interaction with other organizations in their environment, highlighting how these inter-organizational relationships entail power dynamics that must be managed (Hillman et al., 2009; Scott & Davis, 2007; Wry et al., 2013).

Pfeffer and Salancik originally argued that an organization's environment comprises other organizations, and that such organizations have power vis-à-vis a focal firm if they control critical resources (e.g., money, supplies, information, legitimacy) the firm needs. They went on to detail a variety of practical strategies firms could leverage to reduce external constraints related to power-dependence relationships. This theory builds on exchange notions that conceptualize power as the property of a social relationship such that "the dependence of actor A upon actor B is (1) directly proportional to A's motivational investment in goals mediated by B, and (2) inversely proportional to the availability of those goals to A outside of the A-B relation" (Emerson, 1962: 32). By integrating exchange notions of power with open systems approaches to organizations, resource dependence theory provided a unique theoretical orientation that emphasized the need for pragmatic organizational action to loosen social constraints associated with being overly dependent on certain organizations in the environment.

While earlier open-systems research such as work associated with contingency theory (Burns & Stalker, 1961; Emery & Trist, 1965; Lawrence & Lorsch, 1967; Thompson, 1967) emphasized the importance of an organization's environment in shaping organizational design and decision-making, that genre of scholarship tended to invoke rather generic characterizations of organizational environments (e.g., stable versus turbulent). Pfeffer and Salancik (1978) provided a finer-grained conceptualization of an organization's environment as comprising other organizations (e.g., Yuchtman & Seashore, 1967; Zald, 1970). As Wry et al. (2013: 443) asserted, "their implicit assumption was that the major goals of organizational leaders are to avoid dependence on others and make others dependent upon their own organizations ... leaving these decision-makers with the complicated task of managing their environments as well as their organizations." These efforts introduced a variety of new terms that could be used to characterize and study the nature of organizational environments, including organizational sets (Evan, 1972), organizational fields (DiMaggio & Powell, 1983), and organizational populations or resource niches (Hannan & Freeman, 1977).

Even though Pfeffer and Salancik's (1978) book is one of the most highly cited in organization theory, it is often cited ceremoniously without substantive engagement with their initial arguments. Resource dependence also failed to develop into a major paradigm or school of thought that united a wide group of scholars. Instead, resource dependence has provided a core set of ideas that has been embraced by a wide variety of researchers. Wry et al. (2013) highlighted studies that more prominently leveraged resource dependence theory with a variety of somewhat disconnected research foci, including boards of directors (Haynes & Hillman, 2010; Hillman, 2005; Hillman et al., 2007), strategic responses to external pressures (McKay, 2001; Oliver, 1991), and more general studies on power in the context of inter-organizational relationships (Casciaro & Piskorski, 2005; Gulati & Sytch, 2007; Katila et al., 2008).

It is important to emphasize that in contrast to the imagery of battles over resources used in neoclassical economics and population ecology, the social dynamics associated with interorganizational relations provide the key analytical engine for understanding organizational action and developing theory for resource dependence scholars. Thus, while economic resources are a crucial focal point for theorizing resource dependence dynamics, the theory situates competition for resources as socially embedded in interorganizational relations. In addition to providing a bridge between rationalist theories that stress the economic aspects of context and pragmatic theories that focus more on social dynamics, resource dependence theory also provided a bridge to more cultural approaches with an emphasis on how resource dependence dynamics are influenced by the perceptual understandings of organizational actors.

For instance, drawing on Weick's (1969) theory of enactment, Pfeffer and Salancik (1978) suggested that the interpretations and perceptions of organizational actors might be biased due to past experiences and socialization. In addition to drawing on growing interest in perceptions and managerial cognition advanced by the Carnegie School, resource dependence scholars embraced the concept of legitimacy, which, at the time, was conceptualized as the perceived appropriateness and credibility of an organization – often associated with increased resources (Deephouse & Suchman, 2008). This focus on legitimacy, a core concept in institutional theory (discussed in the next chapter), created an enduring bridge between resource dependence theory and the more culturally sensitive institutional theory.

In their excellent review of resource dependence research, Wry et al. (2013) opined that one of the most exciting areas for future research involves bridging to institutional theory; in particular, the institutional logics perspective, a key theoretical variant within institutional theory, that emphasizes how organizational environments are often characterized as institutionally complex – involving a multiplicity of often competing actors, practices, and beliefs. Similar to the behavioral theory of the firm, this interface suggests the need to bridge theories across pragmatic and co-constitutive ontologies. While we have emphasized challenges in moving across ontologies, there are also advantages and opportunities associated with forging new conversations and ideas through this sort of bricolage (Lévi-Strauss, 1966), suggesting theorists might benefit from making use of whatever intellectual ideas they have at hand.

3.4   Embeddedness and networks

While theories such as resource dependence stressed the importance of interorganizational relations, research on networks and embeddedness has sought to develop more formal approaches that can be used to study such relationships, as well as how the entire relational structure of industries and fields shapes the behavior of organizations. However, a tension has emerged between two broad research orientations. One embraces more formalized network analytic approaches that valorize the importance of structure – providing fairly static analyses of how different kinds of nodes are positioned in relation to each other (Mayhew, 1980) – while the other seeks to unpack the dynamics of relational processes (Emirbayer, 1997). In this section, we briefly describe these two camps.

Formal network analysis has diverse roots, but Simmel (1955) provided an early theoretical architecture with his discussion of triadic relationships and the web of group affiliations.

> Triads are, of course, small networks, but they have interesting possibilities. A friend of my friend may be a friend, and an enemy of my friend is likely to be an enemy – but there are more interesting possibilities when my friend acts as a broker (keeping the two of us separate and acting as a conduit), an arbitrator (mediating conflicts between us), or a spoiler (fomenting conflict between us). (Scott & Davis, 2007: 279)

These insights became foundational for the development of network analytic techniques, first in sociometry (Moreno, 1953) and then in formal network analysis programs developed since the 1970s (e.g., Structure, UCInet, Pajek, and the like).

Social network analysis tools often rely on a matrix of data that reveals how nodes (individual actors, people, or things within the network being mapped) are interconnected via ties, edges, or links (relationships or interactions). A multitude of theoretical concepts and related measurements (e.g., centrality, density, structural holes, strength of ties) can be used to characterize the structure of a network and predict how a node's position in a network shapes observed behavior (see Wasserman & Faust, 1994, for a comprehensive overview). While empirical research is as diverse as theory and method, Brass and colleagues have provided useful recent overviews (e.g., Brass, 2022; Brass & Borgatti, 2020; Kwon et al., 2020).

Scott and Davis (2007) argued that while there is no unitary theory of networks, the community of network scholars might be best understood as sharing a worldview. However, we disagree. The universe of network related research is so diverse that we cannot identify a single, coherent worldview. For instance, we believe that an important distinction can be made between research that leverages formal network analysis methods in a more static and structural way, and scholarship that embraces a more dynamic and contextualized approach to the study of networks and relationships and takes a more nuanced view of agency and structure (Tasselli & Kilduff, 2021). Moving in the latter direction, Granovetter (1985) advanced one of the most prominent ideas in the literature – embeddedness – which is associated with the substantivist school in anthropology (Polanyi, 1944). This has provided a kind of meta-theory for network analysts based on the assertion that behavior at any level (individual or organizational) cannot be adequately understood unless one appreciates how behavior is shaped by the structure of social relations, as well as institutions within which a focal actor is situated.

In that groundbreaking statement, Granovetter (1985) provided a trenchant critique of neoclassical economics and Williamson's transaction cost perspective for embracing what he referred to as an undersocialized, or atomized actor explanation of human behavior. While he also criticized many sociological accounts of behavior for providing a structurally deterministic, or oversocialized explanation of human behavior, his approach to the study of network relations implies a much more process-oriented and context-sensitive approach. He argued:

> A fruitful analysis of human action requires us to avoid the atomization implicit in the theoretical extremes of under- and oversocialized conceptions. Actors do not behave or decide as atoms outside a social context, nor do they adhere slavishly to a script written for them by the particular intersection of social categories that they happen to occupy. Their attempts at purposive action are instead embedded in concrete, ongoing systems of social relations. (Granovetter, 1985: 487)

Granovetter's (2017) *Society and Economy* further fleshes out the embeddedness perspective by embracing pragmatism as an ontological anchor for his conceptualization of agency. Given his emphasis on how behavior is situated in a flow of relationships, trust is a central concept. He critiqued economic approaches that attribute trust at the macro level (e.g., between firms) to micro-level processes of socialization determined by nation-state cultures that have been characterized as either "low trust" (e.g., China, France, and Italy) or "high trust" (e.g., Japan, Germany, and the United States). Instead, he argued for more detailed inquiries into "how the nature of trust at a small scale might translate into the capacity to structure larger-scale economic organizations" (p. 85). He also leveraged his earlier research on the strength of weak ties (Granovetter, 1973) to highlight how community-level variation in the nature of networks has implications for whether a person trusts a given organizational leader. Overall, he provided a grand, multi-level approach to study how social networks shape organizational life as an alternative to rational choice economic accounts of socio-economic life that embrace ideal-typical conceptualizations of markets and interests which, as he argued, are incomplete at best, and in many cases, are fundamentally wrong.

The line of work that has been inspired by Granovetter's approach to embeddedness has advanced our understanding of relational dynamics by emphasizing the importance of context, pointing us toward the need to more deeply appreciate the content of behavior and relational ties. For instance, based on ethnographic and survey data tracking behavior over several years, Obstfeld (2005) challenged dominant arguments in the literature that brokers who are situated in advantageous positions (e.g., in structural holes) always behave in opportunistic ways that benefit themselves – what Burt (1992, 2004) referred to as the tertius gaudens orientation. Instead, he showed how those in advantaged structural positions who are involved in organizational innovation behave with a tertius iungens (i.e., more cooperative) orientation by either introducing disconnected individuals or facilitating new coordination between connected individuals. This research elaborated Ibarra's (1993) finding that network centrality provided a basis for mobilizing support for innovation, thereby fostering a more dynamic network perspective on innovation processes.

The scholarship of Powell and colleagues has also greatly advanced our understanding of network dynamics (e.g., Padgett & Powell, 2012; Powell et al., 1996; Powell et al., 2005). In particular, Padgett and Powell (2012) developed a theory of the co-evolution of social networks by focusing on the general problem of emergence and highlighting network mechanisms of organizational genesis. They argued that novelty emerges through spillovers across multiple, intertwined networks related to politics, markets, kinship, and science which shape the topology of the possible, creating a landscape in which new alternatives can be invented. Embracing a deeply historical and relational perspective, they critiqued rational choice economics and actor-centered approaches to innovation, arguing that "in the short run, actors create relations; in the long run, relations create actors" (Padgett & Powell, 2012: 2).

While most network and emebeddness research embraces more of a pragmatic ontology, some of the research in this domain, exemplified by Padgett and Powell, begins to shift toward more of a co-constitutive ontology, albeit one that is more focused on the dynamics of social networks than the cultural processes we discuss in the next chapter. However, given the compatibility between research on embeddedness and cultural perspectives such as institutional logics, there are opportunities for cross-fertilization – as emphasized by Granovetter (2017), who has explicitly bridged these approaches. We believe that such bridging may be particularly useful in enhancing our understanding of the dynamics of entrepreneurial ecosystems (e.g., Shipilov & Gawer, 2020) as well as organizational and institutional fields (e.g., Zietsma et al., 2017).

3.5   Social movements and organizations

While much of the social movements scholarship is grounded in sociology and political science, strong connections have been made to organization theory over the years, with increased cross-fertilization since 2000. While definitions of social movements vary, they generally describe coordinated efforts by groups of individuals and organizations to foment or resist social change. As such, social movements require organizing and often comprise organizations, especially so-called social movement organizations, that seek to frame movement goals, devise tactics and mobilize resources to support goal attainment (e.g., McAdam et al., 1996; McCarthy & Zald, 1977; Snow & Soule, 2009).

Beginning in the 1990s, researchers who study organizations and social movements began to develop a more robust interface between these fields of scholarship. They have increasingly applied insights from organization theory to enhance our understanding of movements, and drawn on ideas and theory from social movement scholarship to broaden our understanding of organizational dynamics (e.g., Clemens, 1993, 1997; Davis & McAdam, 2000; Davis et al., 2005; Davis & Thompson, 1994; Fligstein, 1996; Lounsbury, 2001; Rao et al., 2000; Soule, 1997). This interface has greatly enhanced our understanding of both movements and organizations. We discuss two key focal points of research at this interface – how movements facilitate the creation of new organizational fields and how movements alter or transform the nature of existing fields (Fligstein & McAdam, 2012; Schneiberg & Lounsbury, 2017). It is useful to note that scholars working at this interface have engaged diverse organization theories across the ontologies we emphasize – rational choice, pragmatic, and co-constitutive. However, most research in this genre aligns more with a pragmatic ontology.

Earlier in this chapter we noted how some network scholars (e.g., Padgett & Powell, 2012) have begun to focus on the importance of theorizing and studying emergence. Likewise, this long neglected topic has become a broader focal point for organization theorists (Seidel & Greve, 2017). Since social movement scholarship focuses on processes related to social change, it is perhaps no surprise that many scholars are exploring the role of social movements in the creation of new organizational fields. However, the movements to create new organizational fields often differ markedly from conventional mass movements (e.g., civil rights, women's rights, LGBTQIA+, Black Lives Matter) documented in the social movements literature. The creation of new industries or markets may involve citizen activists and other activist organizations, but may also include new types of producer organizations that ultimately seek to make money in novel markets.

The literature is filled with empirical exemplars. For instance: Rao (1998) documented how the creation of the consumer watchdog field (with organizations and product rating schemes) was catalyzed by consumer mobilization; Lounsbury et al. (2003) tracked how the environmental movement gave rise to a new recycling industry; and Weber et al. (2008) showed how social movements paved the way for cultural change via the creation of the grass-fed beef market. These kinds of studies not only highlight the role of diverse actors, including nascent producer organizations, but also emphasize that emergence can be a conflict-ridden process; this is in contrast to the depiction of organizational emergence as a slow, evolutionary process (e.g., Aldrich et al., 2020). The change that movements seek often threatens the power of established organizations and other actors, leading to protracted struggles. For example, in the cases of recycling and grass-fed beef, the creation of these new fields and related markets unfolded over a long period of struggle vis-à-vis dominant incumbents in the solid waste and industrial beef fields that were, at least initially, quite resistant to those movements.

It is important to note that in most cases of social movement-driven market creation, conflict and struggle often endure after the focal market is acknowledged to exist. Often, this is because social movements are motivated by values and commitments (e.g., to create a more sustainable and equitable society) that tend to conflict with more commercially oriented market logics that emphasize efficiency and profit. This has led to the development of a literature on moral markets that explores these dynamics in greater depth (e.g., Fourcade & Healy, 2007; Hedberg & Lounsbury, 2021; Lee et al., 2017; McInerney, 2014; Schiller-Merkens & Balsiger, 2019). For instance, McInerney (2014) studied how social justice activists, called "Circuit Riders," pioneered a new market segment aimed at providing information technology services to grassroots and nonprofit organizations in support of social justice efforts. Once successful, large corporations such as IBM, Adobe, and Microsoft entered the market, threatening the initial emphasis on social justice in favor of market-building. However, Circuit Rider activists continued to push their agenda, albeit in a more muted form, developing new social outreach initiatives such as to First Nations communities in Canada with philanthropic support from some of the large corporations that had entered the new market.

This literature on moral markets provides a bridge between research streams on movement-created fields and markets, and movement challenges inside established fields and markets. The research on movements within markets is quite wide ranging. For example, some research tracks broad movements that seek to reform that nature of capitalism such as Schneiberg and Soule's (2005) study of anti-corporate movements in the early 20th-century U.S. insurance field. Attacking powerful corporate trusts, the Grange, Farmers Alliance, and other groups directly opposed for-profit corporate forms of organizing insurance in favor of a more decentralized and cooperatively organized economy of independent producers, farmers and self-governing towns. They were largely successful in convincing legislators to pass anti-trust laws to enable the rise of mutual insurers, breaking the oligopolistic stronghold of dominant insurance corporations.

Other research focuses more on how different kinds of movement activities have enabled corporate reforms, including the rise of B Corporations (Gehman & Grimes, 2017; Lucas et al., 2022), and the adoption of new programs and practices related to corporate social responsibility (CSR), environmental, social and governance practices (ESG), and diversity, equity and inclusion (DEI) (e.g., Briscoe & Safford, 2008; de Bakker et al., 2013; Hiatt et al., 2015; McDonnell & King, 2013; McDonnell et al., 2015; Soule, 2009; Vasi & King, 2012). Some scholars have documented how this movement activity is organized by non-profits who are able to embed the changes they seek in private governance systems connected to rating and ranking schemes (Bartley, 2007). But, as we have noted, movement challengers are always involved in political struggles with incumbent actors (e.g., corporations) who have the resources to resist (Ingram et al., 2010; Rao et al., 2011; Soule, 2009; Yue, 2015). Thus, change-oriented activism is often subject to corporate counter-mobilization efforts including "astroturfing" strategies that aim to create false public perceptions of grassroots support for a policy or product (Walker, 2014; Walker & Rea, 2014). This research also intersects with contemporary scholarship on resource dependence theory that seeks to contribute to a broader understanding of how firms engage in non-market strategies to appease activists and a wide variety of stakeholders (e.g., Briscoe et al., 2018; Hillman & Hitt, 1999). The complex relational dynamics between organizations and activists requires much more focused research attention (Odziemkowska, 2022).

It is important to note that social movement dynamics also play out inside organizations (Briscoe & Gupta, 2016). However, in the context of internal collective action processes, radical activism may be muted when potential activists are also employees who, more often than not, want to keep their jobs. Thus, much so-called insider activism involves what Meyerson and Scully (1995) referred to as "tempered radicals" who seek to refashion organizational policies via more conventional means. Research in this vein also focuses on how employees or occupational actors such as recycling coordinators (Lounsbury, 2001), sustainability managers (Augustine, 2021), LGBTQIA+ employee activists (Creed & Scully, 2000; DeJordy et al., 2020), and diversity managers (Dobbin, 2009) engage in activist behavior to promote wider, societal-level social movement goals. This scholarship often connects to institutional analysis to understand how broader institutional pressures related to societal-level social movements work their way into organizations, facilitating change in and across organizations. This research also has strong potential to link to wider research on work and occupations, professions, and research on organizational change (e.g., Buchter, 2021; Kellogg, 2009).

3.6   Discussion

The pragmatic theories we have discussed – the behavioral theory of the firm, resource dependence, embeddedness and networks, and social movements and organizations – all provide a fruitful contrast to rational choice theories by providing a richer understanding of agency and actors in relation to the structures and forces within which they are situated. This is mainly because rationalist theories tend to abstract away from actors, making simple assumptions about behavior (e.g., self-interested maximization of utilities), whereas pragmatist theories zoom in a bit more on the complexities of actors' interactions with other actors and elements of their environment. Rather than economic aspects of an organization's context, social dynamics are given primacy. In addition, organizations are conceptualized as more interpenetrated with, as opposed to segregated from, their environments.

Given the focus on social dynamics in pragmatic theories, rationalist theorists might argue that the roles of economic processes and self-interest are overlooked. Likewise, co-constitutive theorists might argue that the importance of culture and meaning is a blind spot. Nonetheless, the pragmatic theories we have discussed have had a major influence on organization theory research, and highlight many aspects of the social world that are crucially important, yet often neglected by rationalist and co-constitutive scholars.

The behavioral theory of the firm, for instance, has been incredibly influential in this regard, providing a more behaviorally rich approach to organizational decision-making and behavior that highlights the limits of existing rationalist approaches to organizations. Over time, this program of research has increasingly shifted from intra-organizational dynamics to appreciating how wider environmental dynamics shape and influence the politics of decision-making. As such, this theory has begun to mesh well with co-constitutive theories such as the institutional logics perspective.

Resource dependence theory also has been a staple in the field since its initial development, providing a social perspective on organizational dynamics that foregrounds the role of dyadic, episodic power in shaping organizational behavior. Network research has generalized insights from resource dependence theory to highlight the complexity of network relationships and interactions beyond the dyad. This has led to many fruitful insights, and has highlighted the general importance of understanding organizations not as atomistic actors, but as actors that are enmeshed in a variety of ongoing social relationships. As we noted, some scholars have made the case that organizations are more profoundly embedded in societal contexts, expanding structural network claims to understand the role of cultural processes as well. While more structural approaches to networks may have more affinity with rationalist theories, embeddedness approaches tend to mesh better with co-constitutive theories.

Finally, research on social movements and organizations has highlighted how complex social interactions related to collective mobilization can profoundly affect organizational behavior, as well as how organizations may engage in collective mobilization to create and change organizational industries and fields. We have noted how social movement activism occurs inside organizations, and can provide a motor for organizational change. Like much of the research inspired by pragmatist theories, power dynamics are central, as are cultural aspects such as framing. Again, to the extent researchers aim to analytically embrace both culture and power, scholarship in this area is likely to provide opportunities to bridge to co-constitutive theories. In the next chapter, we shift our focus to co-constitutive approaches to organization theory.

4. Co-constitutive theories

Rationalist and pragmatic theories tend to be actor-centered, focalizing in different ways on actors' decision-making. Co-constitutive theories problematize the nature of actors, drawing attention to the ways in which actorhood is itself an accomplishment shaped by an ongoing interplay with wider cultural processes (Douglas, 1970; Hwang & Colyvas, 2020; Hwang et al., 2019; Meyer, 2010; Ruef, 1999). Accordingly, rather than taking actorhood for granted, co-constitutive theories seek to understand the emergence of different categories of actors, together with the societal consequences of their actions (e.g., Fligstein & McAdam, 2012; Lounsbury & Wang, 2020; Meyer & Vaara, 2020). As Hirschman and Reed (2014: 259) put it: "the kinds of social things that exist now did not always exist and may not always exist in the future." Co-constitutive theorists are interested in documenting and explaining such transformations, together with their consequences for organizations and society.

In terms of ontology, many co-constitutive approaches to organization theory are influenced by the philosophical tradition of phenomenology (for reviews see de Vaujany et al., 2023a; Gehman, 2021a; R. E. Meyer, 2008). Phenomenological philosophy (e.g., Heidegger, 1962; Husserl, 1970; Merleau-Ponty, 2012) has inspired a great deal of research in organization studies, including more micro process-oriented research that privileges subjective human experience in the world (e.g., Langley & Tsoukas, 2016), as well as more macro research focused on how the interests and identities of actors are shaped by broader institutional processes (e.g., Meyer & Jepperson, 2000). Burrell and Morgan (1979) classified phenomenology as occupying an extremely subjectivist position within their analytical scheme. "Such an understanding, however, is flatly wrong. It confuses the transcendental with the psychological, and repeats the mistakes of Descartes and Kant that Husserl explicitly intended to avoid" (Gehman, 2021a: 240; see also Lok & Willmott, 2019). Instead, Husserl understood phenomenology as the study of phenomena as they appear to us, prior to any mediation by signs (Moustakas, 1994; Smith, 2018). Thus, "phenomenology investigates the originary ontological experiences that institute … the sense of being that we possess naturally today" (Lawlor, 2003: 28).

Additionally, phenomenology enables a co-constitutive understanding of context. Phenomenologically speaking, context is not exogenous to experience, but part and parcel of it. As Merleau-Ponty (1964: 25) explained: "the experience of perception is our presence at the moment when things, truths, values are constituted for us; that perception is a nascent *logos*; that it teaches us, outside all dogmatism, the true conditions of objectivity itself." For this reason, co-constitutive approaches stress contextualization, a process whereby "the real and subjectivity are always constituted in relation to the world" (Faÿ & Deslandes, 2023: 197). From this perspective, context is the medium and outcome of action (Giddens, 1984; Lok & Willmott, 2019), co-constituted by the performative efforts of those involved (Garud et al., 2014, 2018; Tsoukas, 2023). In this chapter, we consider several theoretical conversations that, at least in some of their variants, make use of phenomenological precepts. These include institutional theory, sensemaking, and practice theory.

4.1   Philosophical foundations of co-constitutive theories: phenomenology

Phenomenology provides an onto-epistemological basis (i.e., a coherent package of paradigmatic assumptions) for developing an anti-dualist understanding of organizations (Sandberg & Tsoukas, 2011; Tsoukas, 2023). In this regard, phenomenology offers an account of action and agency that is at odds with utilitarianism. Rather than being driven by rational calculation and self-interest (Dreyfus & Dreyfus, 1984), our being-in-the-world is first and foremost a network of meanings, oriented around our concerns (Gallagher & Zahavi, 2008). And, while phenomenology has some common ground with pragmatism (in the sense that both can be thought of as post-Cartesian ontologies), rather than focusing on problem solving, phenomenology emphasizes what Dreyfus (2014) called "skillful coping." As beings, our interest in "things" is driven by social considerations and local values, and toward intersubjectively structured goals (Gallagher & Zahavi, 2008). For instance, viewed phenomenologically, there are right and wrong ways to use things, guided by normative and teleological considerations (Schatzki, 2002). The equipment we skillfully employ also implicates important identity considerations; in a quip, "one is what one does" (Heidegger, 1962: 283).

> To open a *world* in Heidegger's sense requires that the affordances that matter to us and draw us in depend not merely on our needs and previous experience, as with animals, but on what matters to us given our identities, and we are capable of changing our identities and so our world. (Dreyfus, 2014: fn 52)

Although multiple histories of phenomenology could be charted – for instance, Kant, Hegel, and Brentano all used the term phenomenology – the concept's origin is widely attributed to Husserl (Beyer, 2018; de Vaujany et al., 2023b; Moran, 2005; Smith, 2018). Husserl's phenomenology inaugurated a "new idea of philosophy" that sought to describe the origins of the world in non-mundane terms (Lawlor, 2003: 147). In turn, Husserl's former student, Heidegger, applied the phenomenological method to ontology (i.e., the study of being). In so doing, Heidegger "shifted the object of phenomenology from consciousness to worldly familiarity" (Riemer & Johnston, 2017: fn 5). Ultimately, phenomenology "sets up all of twentieth century continental philosophy" (Lawlor, 2003: 147), animating the ideas of Merleau-Ponty, Levinas, Deleuze, Derrida, and others. Of particular relevance to the study of organizations, Husserl had an enormous influence on Alfred Schütz and Berger and Luckmann, and, by extension, the field of sociology more generally (Fay, 2003; Vaitkus, 2000; Scott, 1987; Meyer, 2008). Beyond philosophy and sociology, Husserl also had considerable impact on the development of fields such as cognitive psychology and linguistics (Beyer, 2018).

In terms of its axiological considerations, phenomenology conceives of our equipment, our skillful coping, even mundane and ordinary "things" as "things 'invested with value'" (Heidegger, 1962: 96). In other words, to be is to be concerned, and the world we experience is the world of our concerns (Creed et al., 2022; Gehman, 2021b). One implication of these insights is that our values and morals consist of "unreflective, egoless responses to the current interpersonal situation," the result of "our everyday ongoing ethical coping" (Dreyfus, 2014: 185). Dreyfus views ethical coping as an acquired skill; we move from novice to expert based on our experiences. But unlike pragmatists, such as Dewey, who favor a situated, problem-solving approach to ethical dilemmas (e.g., Dewey, 1960), phenomenology emphasizes ethical skills and the extent to which these may break down (or not). "As ethical skills increase one would expect the expert to encounter fewer and fewer breakdowns. Indeed, phenomenological description suggests that, the greater the experience, the rarer the need for deliberation" (Dreyfus, 2014: 191).

As already noted, at the core of phenomenology is a commitment to returning to things as they appear to us in experience, prior to mediation through signs. This bracketing out of the so-called natural attitude applies especially to scientific concepts (Husserl, 1970). For instance, as it relates to a concept such as "rational choice," a phenomenological stance would imply the need to examine the original experiences that gave rise to such taken for granted assumptions. We can see this process illustrated in Husserl's analysis of the origin of geometry. He asserted that "thanks to our earlier scientific schooling" (Husserl, 1970a: 36), we now take for granted applied geometry and the mathematization of nature. "But if we go back to Galileo ... what came to be taken for granted only through his deed could not be taken for granted by him" (pp. 36–37). Strikingly, Galileo himself eventually took for granted that geometry could produce "self-sufficient, absolute truth" about the world and, in turn, assumed that geometry "could be applied without further ado" (Husserl, 1970a: 49).

Despite becoming taken for granted by Galileo, Husserl argued that the "scientific method ... changes nothing of the essential meaning of the pregiven world" (Husserl, 1970a: 50). The "actually experienced and experienceable world ... remains unchanged ... whatever we may do" (pp. 50–51). Returning to the example of rational choice theory, what phenomenology reveals is the extent to which rational agency is "not only embodied, but individuated" (De Monticelli, 2020: 374). As Callon (1998a: 22) so wryly concluded: "yes, *homo economicus* does exist, but is not an a-historical reality; he does not describe the hidden nature of the human being. He is the result of a process of configuration." As discussed below, it is precisely these processes which the phenomenological attitude seeks to elucidate.

4.2   Institutional theory

Institutional analysis is one of the most prominent theoretical traditions in organization studies (Greenwood et al., 2017). While there is not a single general theory of institutions, the label "institutional theory" is colloquially used to refer to theoretical orientations across the behavioral sciences (e.g., sociology, economics, political science, and organization studies) that emphasize the role of durable social traditions and arrangements. The notion of institution is broad – generally referring to stable reproducible forms of behavior undergirded by regulatory, normative or cognitive forces, and transported by different carriers including cultures, structures and routines (see Scott, 2014, for a comprehensive overview). Ocasio (2023) emphasized that institutions comprise taken-for-granted systems of roles and interactions taking shape in and across multiple levels of analysis, requiring attention to macro-micro linkages (see also Steele et al., 2021).

Institutional theory has deep foundational roots in sociology and social theory dating back the writings of Weber and Durkheim, the more interactional theories of Cooley (1902) and Mead (1934), and the mid-20th-century "old institutionalism" associated with Selznick, Merton, and Stinchcombe (Glynn & D'Aunno, 2023). We focus on more contemporary developments emanating from sociology in the 1970s, often referred to as the "new institutionalism" and, more recently, organizational institutionalism (Greenwood et al., 2017). Building on the emergent cultural turn in the social sciences and humanities, new institutionalism has provided a profoundly cultural approach to studying the effects of organizational environments on organizational decision-making and practice (DiMaggio & Powell, 1991; Meyer & Rowan, 1977). Emphasizing "collective rationality," this approach developed in opposition to rationalist approaches to organizations that emphasized the role of efficiency and valorized the role of interest-driven individual behavior. Institutionalists argue that what counts as rational is itself shaped by socially validated understandings and taken-for-granted assumptions. As Schneiberg and Clemens (2006) succinctly put it, institutional theory is an anti-reductionist approach that seeks to explain the behavior of organizations and other actors as resulting from contextual effects rooted in wider institutional systems such as fields and world society.

While institutional theory has strands with a more pragmatic focus, a number of scholars have highlighted its phenomenological origins (e.g., Jepperson, 1991; J. W. Meyer, 2008; R. E. Meyer, 2008; Ocasio, 2023; Scott, 1987, 2014). In other words, a core co-constitutive thread runs through much of its development in organization theory that embraces social constructivism (Berger & Luckmann, 1967) and phenomenology (R. E. Meyer, 2008), problematizing the nature of actors and elucidating the socio-cultural sources of their behavior (Dobbin, 1992; Meyer et al., 1997; Meyer & Jepperson, 2000). Renate Meyer (2008) traced the relationship between neoinstitutional theory and phenomenology in depth, arguing that institutional analysis has deep roots in the phenomenological sociology of knowledge (Berger & Kellner, 1984; Berger & Luckmann, 1967; Schutz, 1967; Schutz & Luckmann, 1973, 1989) and related European traditions such as Scandinavian institutionalism (Czarniawska & Joerges, 1996; Sahlin-Andersson, 1996). These traditions maintain that individuals are born into a socio-historical a priori (Luckmann, 1983) that provides "institutionalized typifications, frames of interpretation, actor positions, patterns of action, etc., and thus delineates the boundaries and the 'horizon' within which people can meaningfully act – and beyond which it is impossible to see or understand" (Meyer, 2008: 519).

The co-constitutive approach was strongly evident in the phenomenologically inspired neoinstitutional approach of John Meyer and colleagues, often referred to as world society theory (e.g., Bromley & Meyer, 2015; Dobbin, 1992; Dobbin et al., 1993; Meyer et al., 1997; Meyer & Scott, 1983; Scott & Meyer, 1994). Focusing on explaining formal organizational structure and its decoupling from work practice, Meyer and Rowan (1977: 341) argued that "institutionalized rules are classifications built into society as reciprocated typifications or interpretations (Berger & Luckmann, 1967: 54). ... Institutions inevitably involve normative obligations but often enter into social life primarily as facts which must be taken into account by actors." Commending the phenomenological heritage embedded in the scholarly corpus of world society research (e.g., Meyer et al., 1987; Meyer & Jepperson, 2000), Renate Meyer (2008: 520) argued:

> the reciprocity of the typified, scripted action and the type of actor who is expected to perform the script is central to the notion that institutions are constitutive for social actors and actorhood and for organizational institutionalism's claim against rational choice models that actors' preferences and interests are tied to and do not precede the institutional order they belong to.

The world society project evolved to focus more broadly on how modern actors are ongoing cultural constructions emanating from the secularization of religion and the embrace of broad Enlightenment ideas related to progress, justice and individualism that underpin the liberal capitalist-democracy model (Meyer & Jepperson, 2000). This program of research has traced how the development of modern global institutions entailed the construction of world cultural scripts and templates around democracy, human rights, science, education, and environmentalism that have profoundly shaped the structure and behavior of nation-states, organizations, and individuals across the globe (Schofer et al., 2012). In this literature, scholars argue that these trends have become particularly prominent in the post-World War II era with the creation of the United Nations and other prominent international governance bodies and associated infrastructure, thereby enabling the rise and spread of the liberal international order. In recent writings, these scholars have begun to turn their attention to geopolitical challenges that threaten global society (Lounsbury & Wang, 2020).

A major focus in the early development of institutional analysis was legitimacy, documenting how organizations gain legitimacy by conforming to (or becoming isomorphic with) institutionalized practice models (or rationalized myths) which become key aspects of the cultural environments in which organizations are embedded (Meyer et al., 1987; Meyer & Rowan, 1977; Meyer & Scott, 1983). Spurred by the question "What makes organizations so similar?" DiMaggio and Powell (1983) diverted attention away from market competition and toward the notion of fields to explain emergent similarities among organizations. They prominently argued that "the causes of bureaucratization and rationalization have changed" (DiMaggio & Powell, 1983: 171) and that highly structured fields generate a profound legitimacy imperative resulting in isomorphic pressures that lead to organizational homogeneity via coercive, mimetic, and normative forces. Similarly, building on Weberian ideas about the sources of formal organizational structure, Meyer and Rowan (1977) offered novel arguments about how rationalized collective meanings – what they called rationalized myths – are utilized by organizational managers to construct symbolic structures that enable legitimacy. As structures and practices become common across groups of organizations, they are said to have become institutionalized.

Empirical research in institutional theory in the 1980s and 1990s focused a great deal on uncovering various mechanisms related to institutionalization processes, including isomorphism and organizational legitimacy, generating a virtual cottage industry of studies on the diffusion of practices (Strang & Soule, 1998). However, by the end of the 1980s, critiques began to emerge about the dominant theoretical and empirical emphasis on isomorphism, which downplayed agency, microprocesses, and organizational variation (DiMaggio, 1988; Greenwood & Hinings, 1996;

Hirsch & Lounsbury, 1997). This first led to a new emphasis on institutional entrepreneurship and change (e.g., Battilana et al., 2009; Hardy & Maguire, 2008), and subsequent conversations on institutional work (Lawrence et al., 2013) and social symbolic work (Lawrence & Phillips, 2019), as well as the development of the institutional logics perspective (Thornton et al., 2012).

The institutional logics perspective is arguably one of the most important variants of contemporary institutional theory, shifting attention away from isomorphism and toward the heterogeneity of collective rationalities embedded in institutional logics (Thornton et al., 2012). Building on the groundbreaking work of Friedland and Alford (1991), Thornton and Ocasio (1999: 804) defined institutional logics as "the socially constructed, historical pattern of material practices, assumptions, values, beliefs, and rules by which individuals produce and reproduce their material subsistence, organize time and space, and provide meaning to their social reality." Thornton, Ocasio, and Lounsbury (2012) provided a general theoretical conceptualization of ideal typical logics associated with seven institutional orders – state, family, corporation, community, religion, market, and profession – each comprising elements that vary across several dimensions (e.g., root metaphors, sources of legitimacy, basis of attention, etc.) and providing governance for the constitution and maintenance of logics. The elements that congeal to form logics are conceptualized as resources that, like "cultural tools" (Swidler, 1986), can be strategically employed by people as they engage in and negotiate the challenges of everyday life (McPherson & Sauder, 2013). Thus, each ideal typical logic (e.g., the religious logic) is not monolithic, but can have an indefinite variety of instantiations in concrete situations since the elemental composition of logics can differ across time and space.

In line with world society theory, the institutional logics perspective embraces a strong co-constitutive orientation (Lounsbury & Wang, 2020). Early empirical research on institutional logics focused on temporal shifts in dominant logics (i.e., the collapse and replacement of prevailing logics) and consequences for organizations and fields (Haveman & Rao, 1997; Lounsbury, 2002; Rao et al., 2003; Thornton, 2004; Thornton & Ocasio, 1999). Over time, scholars have increasingly focused on the sources and consequences of institutional complexity, or the co-existence of multiple (often competing) logics (Greenwood et al., 2011; Ocasio et al., 2017). For instance, some people and organizations try to compartmentalize their practices to avoid pressures associated with a conflicting logic, or attempt to develop new practices that are compatible with the expectations and prescriptions of multiple logics (e.g., Almandoz, 2012; Besharov & Smith, 2014; Dunn & Jones, 2010; Pache & Santos, 2013). Scholars have also begun to examine how the impacts of institutional complexity may be filtered by contextual contingencies, including other logics (Lee & Lounsbury, 2015; Zhao & Wry, 2016). Lounsbury, Steele, Wang, and Toubiana (2021) reviewed recent literature on institutional logics and argued for more research on the cohesion, durability and governance of logics, as well as how values and emotion shape their dynamics.

Given the importance of institutional theory and its application across multiple domains of focus, we wanted to briefly highlight some areas of research that we find particularly exciting. For instance, research on institutional complexity has importantly influenced the development of scholarship on hybrid organizing as a way to cope with competing logics that are core to an organization's identity (e.g., Besharov & Mitzinneck, 2020; Cappellaro et al., 2020; Dalpiaz et al., 2016; Gümüsay et al., 2020; Smith & Besharov, 2019). These issues are particularly salient in social enterprises that are betwixt and between variants of market and community social welfare logics (e.g., Battilana & Dorado, 2010; Battilana & Lee, 2014; Dacin et al., 2011; Tracey & Phillips, 2016).

Under such conditions of logic conflict, interactions in and around organizations can get heated – that is, fueled by emotion (Jakob-Sadeh & Zilber, 2019; Toubiana & Zietsma, 2017). In recent years, scholars have paid increased attention to the interrelationship of emotions and institutions (see Voronov & Vince, 2012; Zietsma et al., 2019). Yet, much more theoretical and empirical research is required to understand, for instance, how emotions and institutions are co-constituted. A focus on emotions can also enable us to unpack many other important issues, such as the sources and consequences of stigma, as well as the potential to eliminate it or leverage it as a cultural resource.

A somewhat different application of institutional theory is to the study of work, occupations and professions – what Barley (2008) referred to as "Coalface Institutionalism." This tradition of research is vast, with strong roots in the Old Chicago School that produced penetrating studies of the dynamics of work and workers, which also included attention to issues related to emotion and stigma (e.g., Becker, 1963; Hughes, 1958).

This tradition has enduring relevance (Fine, 1995), and emphasizes not only the importance of performing deep ethnographies of work, but also exploring how the dynamics of work, occupations, and professions play out in and across organizations, providing a crucial set of institutional dynamics that profoundly affect organizations (e.g., Abbott, 1988; Anteby et al., 2016; Howard-Grenville et al., 2017; Nelsen & Barley, 1997; Van Maanen & Barley, 1984).

Overall, institutional theory is a robust family of theories, many of which embrace a co-constitutive orientation and are used to examine a wide variety of problems. As noted throughout the book, institutional theory has provided an especially useful bridge to many other organization theories. This was evident in our discussion of pragmatic theories, but is also true of other co-constitutive theories – sensemaking and practice theory – which we discuss next. As we note, the profoundly cultural orientation of institutional theory and other co-constitutive theories that endogenize organizational environments make it much more challenging to build bridges to more positivist-oriented rationalist theories.

4.3   Sensemaking

While traces of the idea of sensemaking can be found in varied scholarly discourses such as ethnomethodology, for scholars who study organizing, the writings of Karl Weick have been centrally responsible for its development as a theoretical area for research and development. First mentioned in his classic book, *The Social Psychology of Organizing* (Weick, 1969), the idea of sensemaking emphasizes the need to understand the centrality of interpretation and meaning in organizational processes that are inevitably fraught with ambiguity and equivocality. In *Sensemaking in Organizations*, Weick (1995) highlighted seven key properties of sensemaking, noting that it is grounded in identity construction, retrospective, enactive of a sensible environment, social, ongoing, focused on and by extracted cues, and driven by plausibility rather than accuracy.

Reversing rationalist arguments about how interest-driven cognition drives behavior, Weick (1995: 25) asked, "How can I know what I think until I see what I say?" In their overview of the literature, Maitlis and Christianson (2014: 58) argued:

> Sensemaking – the process through which individuals work to understand novel, unexpected, or confusing events – has become a critically important topic in the study of organizations. When organizational members encounter moments of ambiguity or uncertainty, they seek to clarify what is going on by extracting and interpreting cues from their environment, using these as the basis for a plausible account that provides order and "makes sense" of what has occurred, and through which they continue to enact the environment.

A key point is that sensemaking not only involves individual interpretive processes, but how those processes are socially shaped, and how the actions of focal actors shape the perceptions and behaviors of others. Thus, there is an ongoing, reciprocal social dynamic associated with enactment, sensegiving, and sensemaking.

One of the most famous empirical papers on sensemaking is Weick's (1993) analysis of the 1949 Mann Gulch fire in which 13 of 16 firefighters died. The firefighter group was analyzed as a minimalist organization, whose routines were radically disrupted by what Weick referred to as a cosmology episode in which a sudden loss of meaning occurs – leading to the loss of mindful sensemaking, panic, and ultimately, tragedy; such processes have come to be referred to as sensebreaking (e.g., Mantere et al., 2012; Pratt, 2000). Weick (1993: 633–644) stated that "a cosmology episode feels like vu jàdé – the opposite of déjà vu: I've never been here before, I have no idea where I am, and I have no idea who can help me." This occurred because the routine fire they expected – referred to as a 10 o'clock fire – turned out to be quite different and more dangerous, ultimately eroding the unit's ability to coordinate effectively to save themselves. Weick noted how the foreman, Dodge, tried to save his crew by lighting a fire and asking them to join him; but most of the crew ignored him, ran in panic, and ended up burning to death.

This is an unusual paper in that Weick leveraged someone else's research on the Mann Gulch disaster to generate new insights about sensemaking processes in organizations. He emphasized how a focus on sensemaking processes conflicts with orthodox, rationalist approaches to decision-making. Weick's approach aligns with that of Jim March who emphasized that decision-making preferences are often inconsistent and unstable, as well as politically shaped, as we brought up in our discussion of the behavioral theory of the firm (e.g., Cyert & March, 1963). In contrast to rationalist approaches to decision-making, March (1989: 14) stated that "decision making is a highly contextual, sacred activity, surrounded by myth and ritual, and as much concerned with the interpretive order as with the specifics of particular choices." While pragmatic theories such as the behavioral theory of the firm tend to be more actor-centered, they have more affinity with co-constitutive approaches than with rationalist approaches, highlighting the richer possibilities for integration across pragmatic and co-constitutive ontologies in organization theory.

In his paper on the Mann Gulch fire and other work (e.g., Weick, 1988, 1990), Weick aimed to study breakdowns in sensemaking to develop a richer understanding of how organizations can become more reliable and resilient by becoming more improvisational and acting with wisdom. In recent years, the sensemaking literature has grown to focus on the social processes through which sensemaking is accomplished (Maitlis, 2005) – that is, through language (e.g., Cornelissen, 2012; O'Leary & Chia, 2007), narrative (e.g., Brown & Humphreys, 2003; Patriotta, 2003; Sonenshein, 2010), and other discursive practices (e.g., Balogun, 2003; Rouleau & Balogun, 2011). Maitlis and Christianson (2014: 67) noted that sensemaking is more of a perspective than a theory, with a variety of definitions and analytical foci, but offered a useful synthetic definition of sensemaking as "a process, prompted by violated expectations, that involves attending to and bracketing cues in the environment, creating intersubjective meaning through cycles of interpretation and action, and thereby enacting a more ordered environment from which further cues can be drawn."

As noted earlier, this literature is focused not only on reactions to events or crises that lead to breakdowns in sensemaking, but also on how actors shape others' sensemaking processes, for example, via sensegiving (e.g., Gioia & Chittipeddi, 1991). Weick emphasized how agency drives sensemaking processes; in opposition to rationalist processes, action in the world facilitates understanding the world, including who you are and what your interests might be. As Weick (1988: 307) asserted: "action precedes cognition and focuses cognition." It is the dual and reciprocal emphasis in the literature on action and prospective sensegiving on the one hand, and retrospective sensemaking on the other, that undergirds the co-constitutive ontology of this perspective.

However, this perspective tends to be leveraged in research that is relatively micro in orientation – focused on deep case studies of particular organizations, groups or individuals. As Weber and Glynn (2006: 1639) noted, sensemaking tends to focus on "local practices," ignoring "the role of larger social, historical or institutional contexts." Taylor and Van Every (2000: 275) similarly suggested that "what is missing is an understanding of the organization as a communicational construction or an awareness of the institutionalizing of human society that accompanies organization with its many internal contradictions and tensions." Of course, scholars have explored the role of sensemaking processes in enacting organizational environments (Daft & Weick, 1984) and have tried to bridge sensemaking and institutional theory in a few isolated studies (e.g., Anand & Peterson, 2000; Kennedy, 2008; Nigam & Ocasio, 2010), but much more could be done to bridge these theoretical conversations. Weber and Glynn (2006: 1640) argued that more effort needs to directed to exploring how institutions not only constrain cognition and behavior, but "also prime, edit and trigger sense-making."

In addition, we believe that more research needs to be done on how sensemaking processes reshape institutions in both evolutionary and revolutionary ways. In thinking about the interplay of sensemaking and institutions, it is also useful to contemplate the role of power in both episodic and systemic variants (e.g., Maitlis & Lawrence, 2007; Schildt et al., 2020). For instance, Schildt, Mantere, and Cornelissen (2020) theorized the various ways in which power operates in four archetypal sensemaking processes – automatic (preconscious and committed), improvisational (preconscious and provisional), algorithmic (conscious and committed), and reflective (conscious and provisional). By explicitly focusing on different forms of power dynamics, sensemaking research could provide a better bridge not only to institutional theory, but also to other pragmatic theories that more centrally theorize and empirically study the sources and consequences of power.

4.4   Practice theory

In contrast to actor-centered theories, practice theory scholars valorize practice as the primary unit of analysis and advocate for "a distinct social ontology: the social is a field of embodied, materially interwoven practices centrally organized around shared practical understandings" (Schatzki et al., 2001: 3). Imagining the social world as comprising a web of practices, some have argued that certain approaches to practice provide a flat ontology that dispenses with conventional social scientific approaches that conceptualize the world as composed of levels of analysis (e.g., individual, organization, and macro social system). As Schatzki (2001: 1) argued, a practice-centered approach provides a theoretical foundation to "free activity from the determining grasp of objectified social structures and systems, to question individual actions and their status as the building-blocks of social phenomena, and to transcend rigid action-structure oppositions."

There is no single practice theory. Instead, a focus on practice has seeded a family of theories (Sandberg & Tsoukas, 2016) most popularly associated with the works of Bourdieu (1977), Giddens (1984), and Schatzki (2002). Such theories of practice tend to be rooted in phenomenology, especially influenced by the philosophical writings of Heidegger and Wittgenstein, but often promote slightly different definitions of and orientations toward practice (e.g., Nicolini, 2011; Nicolini & Monteiro, 2016). Reckwitz (2002: 249) provided a useful definition of practice as:

> a routinized type of behavior which consists of several elements, interconnected to one other: forms of bodily activities, forms of mental activities, "things" and their use, a background knowledge in the form of understanding, know-how, states of emotion and motivational knowledge.

Echoing Heidegger's notion of equipment, material things or objects are not reduced to objective or functional features, but are conceptualized as indispensable and equal to know-how to carry out particular social practices (e.g., Lê & Spee, 2015).

Importantly, practice theories highlight the co-constitutive aspect of structure and action; that is, social structures emerge from the situated action they also condition (e.g., Sandberg & Tsoukas, 2011). Situated action shapes and is shaped by shared understandings regarding forms of socially meaningful activity that are relatively coherent and established. In organization theory, practice theory has broadly informed a wide variety of theoretical conversations, but tends to be leveraged in the ethnographic study of micro intra-organizational processes (e.g., Dougherty, 1992; Nicolini et al., 2003; Orlikowski, Yates et al., 1995; Spee, 2020). Practice theory also has transformed how we understand cultural processes in and around organizations. While research on organizational culture as a monolithic force (e.g., Schein, 1985) had begun to stagnate by the mid-1980s, practice theories embodied in notions such as "culture as toolkit" (Swidler, 1986) revitalized the study of culture as a more dynamic and heterogeneous strategic resource (e.g., see Weber & Dacin, 2011). We discuss several theoretical conversations that have been influenced by practice theory, including strategy-as-practice (e.g., Golsorkhi et al., 2015; Jarzabkowski et al., 2007; Jarzabkowski & Spee, 2009; Kaplan, 2008; Kaplan & Orlikowski, 2013; Vaara & Whittington, 2012; Whittington, 2003), routine dynamics (D'Adderio, 2008; Feldman et al., 2021; Feldman & Pentland, 2003; Glaser, 2017), performativity (Beunza & Ferraro, 2019; Garud et al., 2018; MacKenzie & Millo, 2003; Marti & Gond, 2018), actor-network theory (ANT; Callon, 1986; Czarniawska & Hernes, 2005; Gehman et al., 2013; Latour, 2005; Law & Hassard, 1999), and institutional theory (Lawrence & Suddaby, 2006; Smets et al., 2017; Thornton et al., 2012).

Strategy-as-practice (SAP) research emerged in response to conventional economic approaches to strategy research that ignored the behavioral dynamics of humans in strategy development (e.g., Jarzabkowski, 2004; Whittington, 2006). As Jarzabkowski and Spee (2009: 70) detailed, SAP scholars broadly focus on studying "practitioners (those people who do the work of strategy); practices (the social, symbolic and material tools through which strategy work is done); and praxis (the flow of activity in which strategy is accomplished)." In contrast to mainstream strategy research which tends to focus on large-scale statistical analyses, most SAP researchers are anchored in the practice theory tradition, drawing on qualitative methods including ethnography, discourse analysis, participant observation, and interviews. The emphasis is on exploring strategy-making practices and processes in-depth to highlight the reflexivity of skillful, knowledgeable agents as they navigate complex organizational processes as well as wider cultural influences. As Vaara and Whittington (2012: 298) noted, "SAP studies have therefore extended mainstream strateg[y] research by bringing to light practices that have largely passed unnoticed, and discovering in them effects that previously were hardly imagined."

Practice theories also have come to inform the study of organizational routines, a core conceptual focal point in many organization theories (Cyert & March, 1963; Feldman & Pentland, 2003; March & Simon, 1958; Nelson & Winter, 1982). Commonly defined as repetitive, recognizable patterns of interdependent actions (Feldman & Pentland, 2003), routines are foundational for the functioning of organizations. Catalyzed by the groundbreaking work of Feldman (2000), recent scholarship has increasingly focused on unpacking the dynamics of routines (Feldman et al., 2021; Feldman et al., 2019). Scholarship on routine dynamics has enhanced our understanding of ambidexterity by exploring how organizations deal with competing pressures to standardize versus retain flexibility, drawing special attention to the role of artifacts (Glaser, 2017; Spee et al., 2016).

Underlying a great deal of this research is a commitment to practice theories that focus on the dynamic, co-constitutive interplay between action and social structure (e.g., Bourdieu, 1990; Giddens, 1984; Schatzki, 2002). As Feldman et al. (2019: 4) opined, practice theories:

> seek to explain the consequentiality of action both empirically in what people do – their actions – and theoretically in the premise that the patterning of collective practice that we label as "strategy," "organization," or "routine" is continuously produced within multiple people's actions distributed across time and space (Feldman, 2015, 2016; Feldman & Orlikowski, 2011; Feldman & Worline, 2016). Thus, people's actions cannot be separated from the continuous unfolding or becoming of social order – the patterning – that is brought about within those actions (Langley, Smallman, Tsoukas, & Van de Ven, 2013; Tsoukas & Chia, 2002).

Scholarship on routines connects to wider practice research that has leveraged the notion of performativity to document how individual performances of a practice (or routine) play a key role in developing, reproducing, and altering a set of ideas and practices through variation in its enactment (e.g., Feldman, 2003; Orlikowski, 2000; Orlikowski et al., 1995). More generally, the notion of performativity emerged to capture how language (e.g., speech acts), as well as discourse and theory more generally, can function as forms of social action and promulgate change (Austin, 1962; Butler, 1988, 1993, 1997; Ferraro et al., 2005). The concept of performativity was notably leveraged by Michel Callon (1998b, 2007), who suggested that "economics does not describe an existing external 'economy,' but brings that economy into being: economics performs the economy, creating the phenomena it describes" (MacKenzie & Millo, 2003: 108). MacKenzie and Millo (2003) showed how this kind of performativity operated in the institutionalization of options trading markets as the behavior of traders became coordinated around the use of the Black Scholes call option pricing model. Similarly, Marti and Gond

(2018) showed how actors use theories to produce and shape organizational practices, and Carton (2020) documented how the notion of blue ocean strategy transformed organizational practices.

In alignment with practice theories that embrace a flat, post-Cartesian ontology, ANT posits that all things in the social and natural worlds exist in constantly shifting networks of relationships (e.g., Callon, 1986; Latour, 1987, 2005). Somewhat controversially, ANT scholars argue that non-human actors (e.g., objects and ideas) are just as important as humans in the creation and evolution of the social world. In addition, ANT scholars embrace descriptive as opposed to explanatory approaches to social theory, arguing that abstract social forces do not exist, and therefore cannot be used to explain social phenomena.

While ANT provides perhaps a more radical approach to exploring the role of materiality in social change, other scholars have leveraged practice theory to develop alternative social approaches to the relationship between human and material agency – often referred to as socio-materiality of practice (e.g., Orlikowski, 2007; Riemer & Johnston, 2017; for reviews, see Leonardi, 2011; Leonardi & Barley, 2010; Leonardi et al., 2012; Orlikowski & Scott, 2008). For example, Orlikowski (2000: 367) used insights from practice theory to gain "a deeper understanding of the constitutive role of social practices in the ongoing use and change of technologies in the workplace." More generally, given the growing role of digitalization and the rise of platforms, there is a tremendous opportunity for organization theory to contribute to our understanding of how these changes are transforming organizations and society (Gegenhuber et al., 2022; Khanagha et al., 2022).

Practice theory also has been fruitfully integrated with institutional theory, most prominently in work rooted in the institutional logics perspective, where the very definition of logics incorporates both symbolic beliefs and material practices (Lounsbury et al., 2021; Smets et al., 2017). A growing number of empirical studies at this interface are unpacking how the dynamics of practice relate to institutional change (e.g., Furnari, 2014; Lounsbury & Crumley, 2007; Micelotta et al., 2017; Quattrone, 2015; Smets et al., 2012; Voronov et al., 2022). For example, Lounsbury and Crumley (2007) showed how practice variation driven by performativity can trigger the creation of new logics. Smets, Morris, and Greenwood (2012) extended this work by uncovering how changes in everyday practice were justified and subsequently spread throughout an international law firm and across the legal field. This interface remains in its infancy and provides an especially fruitful avenue for future scholarly work.

4.5   Discussion

In this chapter, we have discussed co-constitutive organization theories, including institutional theory, sensemaking, and practice theory. These theoretical conversations tend to draw more on phenomenology, emphasizing the importance of cultural processes and conceptualizing an organization's environment as endogenous to its behavior. As we have noted, co-constitutive theories are more antithetical to rationalist theories than to pragmatic theories. As such, bridging rationalist and co-constitutive theories is exceedingly difficult due to their opposing ontological commitments. While rationalist theorists would argue that co-constitutive scholars tend to neglect the centrality of economic processes and the role of self-interested behavior, co-constitutive scholars would argue that these are cultural phenomena that must be understood as social constructions. Co-constitutive theories are often criticized for not attending to power. As we have noted, many scholars have attempted to bridge co-constitutive and pragmatic theories, and we are optimistic about the ability of such integrative efforts to provide more comprehensive approaches to the socio-cultural dynamics of organizational life.

In fact, as we have discussed, institutional theory includes pragmatic and co-constitutive forms of scholarship. While such ontological complexity can be problematic, we believe that it can provide integrative opportunities if mindfully understood. One can find similar ontological variation across sensemaking scholarship. Even within Weick's writings, one can find evidence of pragmatism as well as a more co-constitutive emphasis on meaning-making. In addition, practice theory as a meta-category of scholarship has many variants that blur this interface. Indeed, when exploring the details of theoretical research programs and individual scholars, ontological commitments may appear to be ambiguous. Nonetheless, we believe that even though the broad analytical categories (rationalist, pragmatic, and co-constitutive) comprising our typology may be fuzzy, they are broadly useful for understanding differences among organization theories and organization theorists.

In addition, the ambiguity and fuzziness we highlight may be thought of as providing opportunities for new forms of scholarship that bridge different theoretical conversations. We highlighted some overlaps between rationalist and pragmatist theories earlier in the book, but bridging is most evident in the field among and between pragmatist and co-constitutive theories. Nevertheless, it is important to emphasize the potential perils associated with such integrative efforts, as very strident co-constitutive theorists can maintain ontological commitments that remain hostile to more pragmatic approaches that valorize social interaction, and vice-versa.

While we all have our biases and commitments, we would argue that there is value in each of the ontological approaches we discussed, as well as the theoretical approaches comprising them. They reveal different aspects of the world, and, as a result, articulate different lines of action. However, the corollary is that no single theory (or ontological approach) can ever be definitive, and this ultimately undergirds the politics of knowledge that make developing a robust scholarly identity challenging. In the next chapter, we shift our attention to the broad reach of organization theory, and highlight how various types of organization theories have been employed to shed light on empirical dynamics related to entrepreneurship and strategic management.

5.   The broad reach of organization theory

Organization theory is a domain of research with broad relevance across all aspects of society and economy. Thus, it is vital to various disciplines and scholarly fields. While organization theory is most deeply connected to management and sociology, it also has proven useful in political science, economics, anthropology, and various other fields, such as those related to public policy. While we have concentrated primarily on scholarly conversations in management, it is important to recognize the broad reach of organization theory. In sociology, for instance, organization theory has been important across multiple subfields, including the sociology of occupations, professions, and work; economic sociology; political sociology; cultural sociology; and the more general study of inequality.

The Organization and Management Theory (OMT) Division is one of the oldest and largest divisions in the Academy of Management. But the OMT Division's influence stems from more than simply its age or size; organization theories play an important brokerage role between otherwise intellectually disconnected divisions. For instance, by default, Academy of Management membership includes affiliation with two divisions, and for a significant number of scholars, OMT is one of those affiliations. Cross-membership in the OMT Division is particularly common for members of the Entrepreneurship (ENT), Organizational Behavior (OB), Strategic Management (STR), and Technology and Innovation Management (TIM) Divisions, themselves comprising the other top five largest divisions. This cross-membership occurs because organization theory is integral to understanding myriad organizational dynamics such as leadership, human resources, organizational behavior, analytics, governance, digitalization, management analytics, technology, sustainability, innovation, and many other contemporary topics of interest.

To illustrate both the reach of organization theory, as well as the utility of our framework for understanding the intellectual trajectories of adjacent fields such as these, in this chapter, we focus on situating the use of organization theory within the fields of entrepreneurship and strategic management. We selected these two fields because they are substantively important, as well as core focal points for the scholarly identities of many organization theorists. But we might have just as easily examined the influence of organization theory on the fields of organizational behavior or technology and innovation management. For instance, organization theorists have long been interested in micro-macro linkages (e.g., Lawrence & Phillips, 2019; Selznick, 1949). This has entailed deep theorizing about topics such as individual agency (e.g., Green et al., 2009; Hwang et al., 2019; Meyer & Jepperson, 2000), the role of leadership in organizations and society (e.g., Howard-Grenville et al., 2019; Rider et al., 2023; Selznick, 1957), and, as we saw in Chapter 3, occupations, professions, and work more generally (e.g., Anteby et al., 2016; Bidwell & Briscoe, 2010; Kellogg, 2009).

Similarly, organization theorists have a long history of investigating topics related to technology and innovation (e.g., Burns & Stalker, 1961; Cohen & Levinthal, 1990; Leonardi & Barley, 2010). For instance, organization theory has contributed greatly to understanding innovations as diverse as CT scanners (Barley, 1986), satellite radio (Navis & Glynn, 2010), and nanotechnology (Granqvist et al., 2013; Wry et al., 2014), to name just a few. Although these (and many other) cross-cutting topics are vibrant and important, there is simply more research at these interstices than we can review in this concise introduction. Suffice to say that we encourage both emerging and established scholars to continue forging novel connections that push boundaries, such as those at the interface of organization theory and organizational behavior and organization theory and technology and innovation management.

Having set the stage, in the remainder of this chapter, we explore how these interfaces with organization theory have evolved in the case of entrepreneurship and strategic management. Indeed, many organization theory scholars end up focusing on empirical domains such as entrepreneurship and strategy because these topics are central to many faculty positions in business schools – at least in North America. Of course, at the core of entrepreneurship and strategy are organizations, ranging from new ventures to large corporations, which makes organization theory particularly relevant. Probably not surprisingly, the ontological differences we have emphasized are reproduced in other fields of scholarship (and in the classes we teach) where the use of organization theory is central. If scholars are not attuned to such differences, misunderstandings can occur, oftentimes leading scholars to talk past one another. Thus, in this

chapter, we elaborate on how the different ontologies we have discussed –
rationalist, pragmatic, and co-constitutive – compare and contrast in the
context of these two important scholarly domains.

5.1 Organization theory in the study of entrepreneurship

Entrepreneurship has been one of the most rapidly growing fields in management in recent decades. Bromley et al. (2022) tracked the rise of entrepreneurship discourse and practice historically, showing how it began to
grow post-World War II, and then accelerated dramatically after 1980,
together with other indicators associated with the rise of neoliberalism.
Since 1975, it is estimated that in the United States, degree and diploma
offerings on entrepreneurship grew fivefold, and course offerings grew
from around 250 to well over 5,000 (Prior, 2014). The growing allure of
entrepreneurship is a worldwide phenomenon, as policymakers around
the globe have embraced entrepreneurship as a mechanism to address
problems related to innovation, growth, and development in developed,
as well as developing countries (Eberhart et al., 2022a, b; Weiss et al.,
2023).

As an applied field of academic inquiry, entrepreneurship grew in
tandem with these developments. In the Academy of Management, an
entrepreneurship interest group was formed in 1971, and was converted
into a formal division in 1987. One of the first specialty journals in this
domain, *Research Policy*, launched coincidentally in 1971, followed by
Entrepreneurship Theory and Practice in 1976. The premier scholarly
outlet, *Journal of Business Venturing*, debuted in 1985. Although many
researchers trained in business schools self-identify as entrepreneurship
scholars, the complex and wide-ranging nature of entrepreneurialism has
led scholars to take a multidisciplinary approach to the topic (Aldrich &
Ruef, 2006; Gartner et al., 1992) and embrace a diverse array of ontologies
(e.g., Garud et al., 2014).

Until recently, the rationalist ontology in the form of applied economic
approaches to the topic was dominant (Lounsbury & Glynn, 2019).
Neoclassical economics conceptualized the entrepreneur narrowly – as a
"lightning calculator, the individual who rapidly scans the field of alter-

native productive processes and chooses the optimum at any given set of prices" (Arrow, 1983: 15). However, most economic-oriented scholars interested in entrepreneurship have adopted a more dynamic approach inspired by the work of Schumpeter (1934), who envisioned the entrepreneur as a bold-thinking, charismatic leader who could generate disequilibria by combining resources in novel ways, thereby catalyzing a process of creative destruction (e.g., Kirzner, 1973). Although more dynamic, this conceptualization is rationalist in its valorization of the entrepreneur as a cognitive hero who is able to astutely analyze the exogenous economic environment to discover, evaluate, and exploit opportunities for wealth creation (Shane & Venkataraman, 2000; Venkataraman, 1997).

Foss and Klein (2012) raised concerns that this dominant economic emphasis led to a sole-individual bias in the literature, and thus an overly narrow explanatory focus on the psychological or cognitive aspects of opportunity discovery (see also Garud et al., 2014). It has been widely documented that such an individual-level focus, including trait-based psychological approaches to entrepreneurship, have failed to uncover robust linkages among personality characteristics (e.g., the need for achievement), and the incidence of entrepreneurship as well as entrepreneurial performance (Gasse, 1992). This overwhelming focus on individual entrepreneurial heroes (often white males such as Elon Musk and Mark Zuckerberg), of course, neglects the prominence of many aspects of socio-economic life emphasized by pragmatic and co-constitutive approaches, such as the role of teams in entrepreneurial start-ups (Aldrich & Zimmer, 1986; Felin & Zenger, 2009; Ruef, 2010; Ruef et al., 2003; Stewart, 1989) and wider collective action in generating entrepreneurial opportunities (Lounsbury, 1998; Lounsbury et al., 2003; Sine & Lee, 2009; Wry et al., 2011).

In addition to applied economic approaches that valorize individuals, another prominent rationalist organization theory that has been used to study entrepreneurial dynamics is organizational ecology. Influenced by the ecological thrust in organization theory (e.g., Aldrich, 1979), Aldrich and Wiedenmayer (1993) argued that there is value in shifting attention from traits to a more evolutionary focus on rates of startup activity (Pennings, 1982). As noted in Chapter 2, instead of focusing on individual-level rationality, a more rationalist emphasis on rates was most prominently developed by organizational ecologists that focused on how exogenous resource spaces shape the dynamics of organizational populations. This theoretical tradition, which is less prominent today than it was in the 1980s and 1990s, focused considerable attention on how the dynamics of organizational populations shape the founding of new entrepreneurial organizations. As we discussed, ecologists argue that the founding of new firms increases as an organizational population grows and gains legitimacy, and wanes as an organizational population grows beyond the carrying capacity of a particular resource space. This focus on the macro dynamics of organizational creation tends to accord with other macro-economic approaches to industry evolution that focus on environmental conditions, including knowledge spillovers that enable small firms to grow (e.g., Acs & Audretsch, 1990; Audretsch, 1995).

Notably, a broader evolutionary perspective on entrepreneurial dynamics championed by Aldrich and colleagues (e.g., see Aldrich & Ruef, 2006; Aldrich et al., 2020) seeks to provide a more synthetic approach by integrating rationalist research, including organizational ecology and industry evolution perspectives, with more pragmatic and co-constitutive theories. While laudable, we find that such a synthetic approach risks underplaying ontological divides across different kinds of theories and theorizing, making integration quite difficult. Nonetheless, Aldrich and colleagues' efforts have been extremely influential, offering a more comprehensive overview of entrepreneurial scholarship, and highlighting many fruitful opportunities for bridge building.

As we argued in Chapter 3, pragmatic approaches provide a much more nuanced approach to relationships between actors and their environment, stressing the social dynamics of interaction. While all pragmatic theories discussed are relevant to entrepreneurial dynamics, approaches used to study social movements and networks are commonly invoked to shed light on entrepreneurial dynamics. Many studies document how social movement processes enable the emergence of new organizational forms (e.g., Rao, 1998; Ruef, 2000) and industries (e.g., Lounsbury et al., 2003). In contrast to dominant emphases on individual entrepreneurs in earlier literature, a key point of emphasis in such research is that entrepreneurial processes intended to be transformative often require collective action to alter the nature of institutional structures, an insight that has proven to be especially true of socially oriented ventures (Hietschold et al., 2023).

However, among pragmatic theories, network approaches have arguably been leveraged most prominently in the study of entrepreneurship to show how particular entrepreneurs are enabled by the construction of social networks (e.g., Aldrich & Zimmer, 1986). Stuart and Sorenson (2005: 233) provided one overview of the mechanisms through which social networks might influence the entrepreneurial processes of identifying opportunities and mobilizing resources to seize them: "If one thinks of ideas, knowledge, and capital as the central ingredients entrepreneurs must assemble in new venture creation, social relations provide the connections required to unite these ingredients to form new organizations." Thus, they leveraged network theory to develop more grounded explanations about how entrepreneurs can assemble resources to construct and develop new ventures via social relationships. Other scholars in this vein have detailed the impacts of interorganizational networks on entrepreneurial activities, including entrepreneurs' ties to suppliers and distributors (Uzzi, 1997), banks (Uzzi, 1999), and venture capitalists (Stuart et al., 1999). In a sense, this approach enables pragmatic forms of network analysis to connect with more rationalist economic approaches to entrepreneurship emphasizing the identification and development of entrepreneurial opportunities.

In addition, network approaches that substantively embrace the notion of embeddedness (Granovetter, 1985) aim to study the role of social relationships in ways that accord more with historically oriented, co-constitutive institutional theoretic approaches (e.g., Granovetter, 2017; Granovetter & Swedberg, 2018). These approaches connect to foundations Max Weber laid in the development of sociological approaches to entrepreneurship (Ruef & Lounsbury, 2007). Weber's (1930 [1904–1905]) *The Protestant Ethic and the Spirit of Capitalism* is perhaps the most well-known exemplar, with its provocative thesis that worldly asceticism among certain Protestant sects (particularly Calvinists) yielded an ethic of calculability, efficiency, and self-control that was essential to the rise of entrepreneurial capitalism in the 16th and 17th centuries. Since then, there have been many attempts to identify social category groupings, such as those based on religion, race, or ethnicity, that could explain entrepreneurial activity based on close-knit networks (e.g., see Schatzki, 2002, on the medicinal herb business cultivated by a Shaker village in the 1850s). Emphasizing the historically situated and contingent nature of action, a perspective emphasizing social deviance and ethnic marginality was developed in the 1960s, highlighting how entrepreneurs emerge at the periphery of the dominant value system (e.g., Hoselitz, 1963). Shapero and Sokol (1982) detailed many examples of such entrepreneurial groups, including the

Ibos in Nigeria, Antioqueños in Colombia, Bataks in Indonesia, Ilocanos in the Philippines, refugee groups such as the Cubans and Indochinese in the United States, and displaced French colonists from Algeria, Tunisia, and Morocco who have founded thousands of businesses in France.

Thus, the embeddedness tradition (e.g., Granovetter, 1985, 2017; Polanyi, 1944; Zukin & DiMaggio, 1990) emphasizes the interpenetration of economic, cultural, social, and political processes, as well as the socially constructed nature of reality. This shift toward more dynamic, historical research has invigorated the field of economic sociology and the sociology of entrepreneurship, as well as specific topics such as ethnic entrepreneurship. Waldinger et al. (1990), for example, provided a model to explain patterns of ethnic business growth by connecting the analysis of shifting opportunity structures to the ability of various ethnic groups to mobilize resources through their ongoing networks of interaction (see also Portes & Jensen, 1989; Portes & Zhou, 1996). Inherent in this perspective is the fact that commercial entrepreneurship that is solely profit-oriented and devoid of social and cultural content is quite rare.

While the embeddedness approach to entrepreneurship overlaps and bridges to more general institutional theory approaches to the topic, social relationships tend to be more of an emphasis in the former, while cultural processes tend to be more prominent in the latter. More general institutional theory approaches to entrepreneurship also embrace the Weberian legacy, prominently embracing deep historical and contextual analyses, including work on imprinting that commenced with Stinchcombe's (1965) classic statement on the propensity of organizations to retain the structural features adopted by founders. Shifting more towards an emphasis on agency, Eisenstadt (1980) and DiMaggio (1988) separately coined the term "institutional entrepreneurs" to refer to elites who are positioned to create new and shape extant institutional and organizational forms. This catalyzed studies on institutional entrepreneurs (e.g., Battilana et al., 2009; Hardy & Maguire, 2017). However, as we mentioned in Chapter 4, a lot of this work tended to emphasize agency to the neglect of how structures (including cultural processes) constitute actors, including entrepreneurs (Gehman et al., 2022).

Building on institutional theoretic approaches, cultural entrepreneurship theory provides a more pointed co-constitutive approach to entrepreneurial processes (Lounsbury et al., 2019; Lounsbury & Glynn, 2001,

2019; for a review, see Gehman & Soublière, 2017). This was seeded by DiMaggio's (1982, 1986) research on art museums, opera houses, symphony halls, and theaters in 19th-century Boston, showing how urban elites acted as cultural entrepreneurs by creating highbrow organizations that enhanced their standing in society. Lounsbury and Glynn (2001) built on these ideas to conceptualize entrepreneurship as a profoundly cultural process, providing a theoretical research agenda that emphasized attention to how entrepreneurs' identities are co-constituted by their storytelling activities which aim to legitimate their new ventures or initiatives as a way to acquire the resources they need to survive and thrive. Since that groundbreaking article, the literature on cultural entrepreneurship has grown to include a diverse range of studies on entrepreneurship that show how a wide variety of cultural resources are involved in new venture creation and socio-economic change (e.g., Granqvist et al., 2013; Johnson, 2007; Lockwood & Soublière, 2022; Martens et al., 2007; Navis & Glynn, 2010, 2011; Soublière & Gehman, 2020; Soublière & Lockwood, 2022; Überbacher, 2014; Wry et al., 2011; Zhao et al., 2013).

In contrast to rationalist theories of entrepreneurship, cultural entrepreneurship theory emphasizes how actors' interests and identities, as well as material resources and exchange mechanisms are culturally constructed and symbolically leveraged in the course of socio-economic behavior (Swidler, 1986). While less attention is paid to the role of social networks than in pragmatic approaches, there are significant overlaps between this co-constitutive approach and research on embeddedness. In their agenda-setting book, Lounsbury and Glynn (2019) argued that instead of anchoring on the identification and seizure of exogenously given entrepreneurial opportunities, cultural entrepreneurship research suggests the need to study variegated entrepreneurial possibilities that emerge and diminish dynamically in institutional fields. Applying insights from institutional theory and network analytic approaches to the study of fields, they situated entrepreneurial action amidst an ongoing flow of discourse and practice, highlighting how entrepreneurs and their ventures are culturally co-constituted along with flows of ideas and resources. This requires attention to how future-oriented discourse in fields (Augustine et al., 2019; Gümüsay & Reinecke, 2022) shapes the earliest moments of entrepreneurial processes when there is a great deal of ambiguity about the potential value of new venture creation (Hannigan et al., 2022; Hannigan et al., 2022; Rindova & Martins, 2021). In recent years, these pioneering efforts have inspired more avant-garde approaches, such as narrative and performative perspectives on entrepreneurship (Garud et al., 2014, 2018; Lounsbury et al., 2019).

A related, emerging area of research on emancipatory entrepreneurship focuses on how constraints are eased at the individual level to facilitate entrepreneurship, or, more generally, to enhance agency (Rindova et al., 2009). Such emancipatory entrepreneurship is especially important in contexts involving poverty where entrepreneurship may be more necessary to survive (Bacq et al., 2022; Slade Shantz et al., 2018). Much more research is required on these issues, but we especially encourage deep, context-sensitive scholarship that can unpack how microprocesses observed in poverty situations relate to more transnational development pressures, and while well intentioned, often perpetuate forms of colonialism that may generate perverse outcomes.

In sum, while many variants of organization theory are prominently used in the study of entrepreneurship, the ontological differences we have discussed throughout this book are reproduced in this domain of scholarship. In turn, these differences have implications for how we as scholars position ourselves in relation to each other, and how we forge scholarly alliances to advance particular theories and theoretical conversations. As we have argued, bridging between rationalist and co-constitutive theories is the most challenging, but different variants of pragmatist theory have been shown to connect to rationalist and co-constitutive scholarly discourse. Next, we explore the use of organization theories in the field of strategy, uncovering similar dynamics and differences regarding ontological assumptions.

5.2   Organization theory in the field of strategy

While the field of strategy developed slowly over the course of the 20th century, it began to be more formally organized in the late 1960s and early 1970s. Since then, the field of strategy has grown dramatically. The *Strategic Management Journal*, the field's premier publication, was founded in 1980, and since then, several other strategy focused journals have been launched (e.g., *Global Strategy Journal*, *Strategic Organization*, and *Strategy Science*). In 1981, the Strategic Management Society was established, and has since become the premier organization dedicated to the strategic management field, with close to 3,000 members from over 70 countries worldwide. Strategy scholars also comprise one of the largest divisions of the Academy of Management. Initially established as the Business Policy and Planning division in 1971, it became the Business Policy and Strategy division in 1993, and in 2017 changed its name to the Strategic Management (STR) division. As noted at the beginning of this chapter, the STR and OMT divisions are closely intertwined, with a high percentage of overlapping scholars.

Strategy scholarship has historically focused on explaining how firms maximize performance, and more generally, their success or failure (e.g., Rumelt et al., 1994). Hoskisson et al. (1999) described the field as eclectic and multidisciplinary, attracting scholars from various fields such as economics, organization theory, sociology, psychology, and management. As with the applied subfield of entrepreneurship, this has given rise to varied ontological approaches. Below, we provide a broad overview of some key rationalist, pragmatist, and co-constitutive approaches to strategic management, and highlight key tensions that exist across these ontological communities.

Rationalist theoretical orientations abound in strategic management, including those connected to conventional microeconomics, industrial organization economics, transaction cost economics, agency theory, evolutionary economics, and the resource-based view of the firm. We do not review all of these in comprehensive detail, but instead focus on core touchstones of so-called heterodox approaches to economics. Whereas neoclassical economic theories are grounded in the assumption of perfectly competitive markets, most rationalist heterodox economic approaches in the field of strategic management emphasize deviations from perfect market competition and how individual firms might analyze and take advantage of market imperfections to develop and sustain competitive advantage. Much of this work leverages quantitative econometric analyses of various costs and benefits related to market imperfections, including how such imperfections shape the prices of goods and services to enable above normal returns. For instance, the *Economics of Strategy* textbook (Besanko et al., 2015) provides a nice overview of this rationalist terrain, covering core topics related to markets and competition, the make versus buy decision, market entry dynamics and strategic positioning for competitive advantage. Core rational actor assumptions are embraced to direct quantitative cost-based calculations about supply and demand;

the contextual emphasis is on economic factors which are held to be exogenous to organizational action. Although some literature connected to these approaches appears in strategy and management journals, the primary outlets for such research are economics and finance journals.

To begin, industrial organization is a field of economics that has had a major impact of the field of strategy, focusing attention on the strategic behavior of firms, regulatory policy, antitrust policy, and market competition. While neoclassical economics scholars developed theory based on perfectly competitive markets, industrial organization scholars focused on how most markets are imperfect due to transaction costs, limited information, governmental action, monopolistic competition, and barriers to entry for new firms (Scherer & Ross, 1990). They emphasized how a market's structure shapes firm conduct and performance (i.e., the structure-conduct-performance paradigm; SCP) – also known as the Bain/Mason paradigm of industrial organization (e.g., see Bain, 1956, 1968; Mason, 1939, 1957).

Although the SCP paradigm was useful for determining an industry's average profitability, it did not shed much light on the conduct and performance of individual firms. Beginning in the late 1960s and 1970s, some scholars began to redirect attention to firm-specific strategies, focusing on how firms compete in their environment via key decisions regarding economic and non-economic goals, products, markets, marketing, manufacturing, and the like – essentially flipping the industrial organization SCP focus on its head (Andrews, 1971; Learned et al., 1969; see Porter, 1981 for an overview). Michael Porter (e.g., 1985) popularized these developments with his five forces framework that continues to be used in MBA strategy classes. This framework emphasizes how firms can develop optimal strategies through a rational cost-benefit analysis of their exogenous economic environment, theorized to comprise five key forces to be dealt with: the threat of new entrants, the threat of substitutes, the bargaining power of customers, the bargaining power of suppliers, and the intensity of competitive rivalry. While neoclassical economics emphasizes perfectly competitive markets, this approach suggests that firms should avoid such markets, and instead seek to attain above normal returns by positioning themselves in non-perfect markets where they can build and maintain competitive advantage.

While industrial organization economics scholars highlighted transaction costs as a key factor in their analyses, the notion of transaction costs (Coase, 1937, 1960) became a focal point for a broad theoretical research program on its own – most notably associated with Oliver Williamson (e.g., 1975, 1985), as we discussed in Chapter 2. For instance, bridging contract law and economics, with a particular focus on antitrust issues, Williamson (1975) developed a counterintuitive, neoclassical efficiency argument to counter the monopoly power emphasis in the traditional SCP industrial organization tradition. In this vein, his work is most well-known for its contributions to our understanding of vertical integration – the so-called make versus buy decision. In short, decisions regarding vertical integration are made to achieve economic efficiency by minimizing the costs of exchange. This focus on maximizing efficiency by reducing transaction costs continues to provide a focal point for many economically-oriented strategy scholars (Cuypers et al., 2021).

Another type of cost that has provided a theoretical lacuna is related the principal-agent problem, which refers to the conflict between the interests and priorities that one person or entity – the agent – takes on behalf of another person or entity – the principal (Fama, 1980; Jensen & Meckling, 1976). Commonly referred to as agency theory, this approach has been deployed mainly in the context of corporate governance to analyze how managers as agents serve (or do not adequately serve) shareholders as principals. In addition to guiding empirical inquiry, agency theory has been wielded normatively to support controversial practices such as excessive CEO compensation and hostile corporate takeovers, generating critiques that it is a dehumanizing and dangerous theory that ignores its wider impacts (e.g., Ghoshal, 2005; Nilakant & Rao, 1994; Perrow, 1986). Despite its many detractors, some strategy scholars have argued that it can offer unique insight into information systems, outcome uncertainty, incentives, and risk (Eisenhardt, 1989). Agency theory continues to be prominently used in economics, finance and strategy.

Leveraging a powerful critique of the neoclassical economic emphasis on profit maximization and market equilibrium, Nelson and Winter (1982) developed a novel evolutionary approach to how firms and industries change over time. A core concept for them was the notion of routine that aimed to capture several aspects of organizational behavior. They argued that routines function as a kind of organizational memory, providing an important mechanism for storing a firm's know-how. They pointed out that routines are also truces, reflecting the outcomes of conflicts that were resolved and providing standard operating procedures that mitigate against future conflicts. Finally, routines can embed goals. As Nelson and Winter (1982: 112) asserted, "when this is the case, the routine (in its smoothly functioning version) takes on the quality of a norm or target, and managers concern themselves with trying to deal with actual or threatened disruptions of the routine."

This temporal perspective on firm knowledge in the form of routines has been extremely generative in the field of strategic management. For instance, it importantly seeded the development of the dynamic capabilities perspective that focuses on how an organization's basic competencies can be leveraged to establish short-term competitive positions that can be developed into longer-term competitive advantages (Teece et al., 1997). Despite some debates about how to best operationalize dynamic capabilities (Eisenhardt & Martin, 2000), scholars have focused significant attention on how firms can adapt to radical discontinuous change while maintaining capabilities to ensure competitive survival (Helfat et al., 2007). As such, there is cross-over between this more rationalist economic approach and more pragmatic approaches that emphasize the importance of and challenges related to organizational learning (e.g., Cohen & Levinthal, 1990). Interestingly, some scholars advancing the dynamic capabilities approach have been extremely critical of transaction cost economists, arguing that production costs, shaped by firm capabilities, are more important than transaction costs in shaping vertical integration decisions (e.g., Dosi & Marengo, 1994; Kogut & Zander, 1992; Langlois, 1992; Winter, 1988).

The resource-based view (RBV) of the firm provides a complementary orientation to the dynamic capabilities approach in that it focuses attention on the strategic resources (e.g., internal assets, capabilities and competencies) a firm can exploit to achieve sustainable competitive advantage (Barney, 1991). Barney argued that for resources to enable competitive advantage, they should be valuable, rare, imperfectly imitable, and non-substitutable. The implication for managers is to focus on identifying and understanding core competencies, and to engage in efforts to develop, nurture and maintain such competencies. Notably, some argue that the RBV approach has become the dominant paradigm in strategic management, replacing Porter's (1985) emphasis on external considerations such as industry structure.

In thinking about rationalist approaches to strategy as a whole, it is evident that while we find some discord between proponents of different rationalist approaches to strategy, as well as some efforts to bridge between rationalist and pragmatic traditions, from an ontological standpoint, there is more similarity than difference across rationalist theories. They all generally tend to embrace rational actor assumptions in some form and conceptualize an organization's environment as primarily economic and exogenous to the behavior of organizations. While the evolutionary economic perspective together with dynamic capabilities and RBV provide more relaxed assumptions that facilitate bridging to more ontologically expansive theories, their grounding in economic analysis limits how far they can be stretched to incorporate insights from more sociological theories that focalize social and cultural processes.

Moreover, although rationalist approaches to strategy have arguably been historically dominant in mainstream strategy research and teaching, pragmatic and co-constitutive approaches have been on the rise. Important pragmatist approaches to strategy include stakeholder theory, the behavioral theory of the firm, and network theory. In contrast to rationalist approaches to strategy that focus narrowly on the firm or the relationship of the firm and its managers to shareholders, stakeholder theory emphasizes that organizations are embroiled in social interactions among multiple constituencies, including employees, suppliers, local communities, creditors, and other key actors (Freeman, 1984). As such, it provides a more socio-political approach to firm strategy that integrates insights from various other theories, including network analysis (Rowley, 1997), institutional theory (e.g., Greenwood et al., 2017), resource dependence (e.g., Hillman et al., 1999) and social movement theories, which highlight how organizations are embroiled in political environments that contain a multiplicity of diverse relationships (Scherer & Palazzo, 2007; Werner, 2012).

For instance, Briscoe et al. (2018) highlighted the fertility of integrating social movement theory with stakeholder theory and scholarship focused on non-market strategy. This effort builds on emerging directions in business and society scholarship focused on sometimes contentious relationships between business and various other civil society actors. This new strand of organization theory seeks to understand the dynamics of these relationships and how they create new opportunities for progressive organizational change (Briscoe & Gupta, 2016). This direction for research is particularly promising and has already contributed to a broadening of strategy research well beyond a narrow focus on financial performance, to include a vibrant literature on firms' social performance.

In recent years, there also has been growing interest in leveraging the behavioral theory of the firm to expand the scope of strategy research (Gavetti et al., 2012; Greve & Zhang, 2022). As noted in Chapter 3, ongoing developments around performance feedback theory have important implications for strategy (e.g., Gaba & Joseph, 2013; Kotiloglu et al., 2021; Kuusela et al., 2017; Ref & Shapira, 2017). More generally, because the behavioral theory of the firm focuses on the social dynamics of organizational decision-making, it is broadly relevant to strategic decision-making. Moreover, as signaled by the efforts of social movements, non-market strategies, and stakeholder theory scholars, there is increased interest in a wider variety of organizational goals and outcomes in strategy beyond financial performance. Growing interest in the behavioral theory of the firm also dovetails with more general interest among strategy scholars to focus more deeply on the mechanisms underlying predictions regarding firm actions and outcomes (e.g., Felin et al., 2015). Greve and Zhang (2022) asserted that it would be particularly valuable for scholars to focus on how the content and dynamics of an organization's structure, decision-makers, history, and operating environment shape strategic decision-making. Using historical methods, for instance, Pillai et al. (2020) examined the extent to which early automobile manufacturers learned from what they termed "economic experiments," leading them to hypothesize that such strategic pivots served as the origins for firm strategy and competitive advantage.

Network theory is also being increasingly integrated into strategic management. While traditional strategy approaches are often rooted in economic theories and the underlying assumption that organizations are autonomous actors operating in an exogenous environment (e.g., see Porter, 1980), network theorists stress how organizations are inter-connected and embedded in networks of relationships (Håkansson & Snehota, 1989). Also, strategy approaches such as the RBV of the firm emphasize the importance of internally controlled resources, providing a very limited understanding of how extended networks of firms simultaneously cooperate and compete, and thus must cultivate a variety of organizational relationships to gain access to needed resources (Sanchez & Heene, 1997). Thus, interorganizational relationships and networks are inevitably a strategic issue for firms and can provide a key source of sustainable competitive advantage (e.g., Gulati et al., 2000). As we have stressed in this book, the pragmatic ontology articulated in network theory provides a distinct but useful starting point for understanding how organizations strategically negotiate with other actors in their environments. To embrace this approach to strategy, scholars must acknowledge that the dichotomous economic focus on market versus hierarchy is far too limiting, and that most organizations are network-based entities embedded in ongoing social relationships with a variety of actors (Powell, 1990).

Likewise, co-constitutive organization theory approaches are increasingly influencing strategic management, focusing more attention on the role of cultural processes (e.g., Pollock et al., 2019; Rindova et al., 2011). Here we highlight the contributions of practice theory and institutional theory. On the practice theory side, the recent growth of strategy-as-practice (SAP) scholarship has importantly drawn attention to the actual practices of strategy making (e.g., see Golsorkhi et al., 2015; Jarzabkowski et al., 2007; Jarzabkowski & Spee, 2009; Whittington, 2006). This research tradition built on the more behaviorally focused strategy-as-process research tradition (e.g., Mintzberg, 1978; Pettigrew, 1973, 1992; Van de Ven, 1992) which emphasized how "strategic management is a process that deals with the entrepreneurial work of the organization, with organizational renewal and growth, and more particularly, with developing and utilizing the strategy which is to guide the organization's operations" (Schendel & Hofer, 1979: 11). As we noted in Chapter 4, SAP research initially developed in response to conventional economic approaches to strategy research that ignored the role of "practitioners (those people who do the work of strategy); practices (the social, symbolic and material tools through which strategy work is done); and praxis (the flow of activity in which strategy is accomplished)" (Jarzabkowski & Spee, 2009: 70). Because the practice theory tradition is deeply rooted in an analysis of cultural processes, SAP scholarship has uncovered aspects of strategy-making bracketed by standard approaches to the topic that ignore wider cultural processes related to how strategy practices emerge and change. SAP research highlights the fine-grained socio-cultural dynamics of strategy making, providing a stark contrast to economic approaches that assume strategy making is a rationalist process, unfolding as if it were designed and executed by a computer (e.g., Jarzabkowski & Kaplan, 2015; Jarzabkowski et al., 2016).

Related research also has expanded research on routines beyond evolutionary economic conceptualizations (e.g., Nelson & Winter, 1982)
to understand their performativity and dynamism (D'Adderio, 2008;
Dittrich et al., 2016; Feldman, 2000; Feldman et al., 2019; Feldman &
Pentland, 2003; Glaser, 2017). For instance, Feldman and Pentland (2003)
adopted Latour's (1986) distinction between ostensive and performative
understandings of power, suggesting that routines likewise have ostensive (i.e., standard operating procedures, taken-for-granted norms) and
performative (i.e., improvisation, situational) aspects. Emphasizing the
performative aspect of routines, D'Adderio (2008) theorized the role
of artifacts and distributed agency in shaping routine dynamics. More
recently, Glaser (2017) examined what he called "design performances,"
through which organizations can design artifacts to intentionally influence routine dynamics. More generally, his work contributes to an
understanding of how organizations can create strategy tools that are
responsive to dynamic environments.

Institutional theory also has had an increasing impact on strategy scholarship by focusing on how organizations as actors are interpenetrated with
their wider environments which profoundly shape organizations' strategic actions. Zhao et al. (2017) highlighted how the substantive integration
of institutional theoretic ideas in the strategy literature has grown since
the 1980s – much of it related to the study of categorization processes
and optimal distinctiveness. At the core of this literature is a focus on
how firms strategically manage competing pressures to be both similar
to and different from other organizations in an industry or market (e.g.,
Deephouse, 1999; Durand & Calori, 2006). While traditional approaches
to strategy have emphasized the importance of difference to competitive
advantage, institutional theorists have alternatively shown that similarity
to peer organizations (i.e., isomorphism) has benefits related to legitimacy
and the concomitant avoidance of performance penalties associated with
deviance from existing norms, expectations and practices (e.g., DiMaggio
& Powell, 1983). Building on Brewer's (1991) ideas about how individuals
forge unique identities amid strong normative pressures to conform,
a broad literature has emerged to address the sources and consequences
of firm-level optimal distinctiveness – which generally refers to how firms
resolve these dual paradoxical pressures to simultaneously be similar to
and different from peer organizations (e.g., Zhao, 2022; Zhao et al., 2017;
Zhao & Glynn, 2022; Zuckerman, 2016).

This literature has grown in tandem with the strong cultural emphasis in the literature on categorization dynamics. Recent interest in categorization was sparked by the work of Zuckerman (1999), who documented how categories anchor organizational identity and role conformance, and strategic efforts that span categories can lead to the inattention of key audiences and concomitant penalties – in his case, devaluation of a firm's stock price. Thus, organizations that do not easily fit into categories (e.g., novel firms) may find it difficult to be recognized and "counted" (Kennedy, 2008). More recent research on categorization has highlighted that penalties associated with category spanning may be mitigated (Hsu et al., 2012; Leahey et al., 2017; Ruef & Patterson, 2009; Zhao et al., 2013) or even rewarded (Wry et al., 2014). Overall, this literature has suggested that categories, as culturally constructed competitive niches, importantly shape the identities and interests of actors. The language of categories has begun to replace the language of industries and markets in a substantial proportion of work at the interface of organization theory and strategy.

5.3   Discussion

In this chapter, we have documented how organization theory is used as a resource to shed light on key aspects of other management subfields such as entrepreneurship and strategy. In doing so, we have highlighted how the ontological differences we have delineated throughout the book – rationalist, pragmatic, and co-constitutive – reproduce themselves in other fields of scholarship, and provide a foundation for scholarly identity-making. Entrepreneurship and strategic management are not only important domains of scholarship, but also core areas of teaching for organization theorists. As such, it is important to consider how scholars' ontological commitments shape what and how they teach, ultimately influencing the minds of students in their classrooms.

This is important to consider, given that rationalist economic approaches tend to be dominant in the teaching of entrepreneurship and strategy – at least in North America. If students cum practitioners go into the world valorizing self-interest maximization over the dynamics of social relationships or cultural processes, how will the world we live in be affected? Performativity theory suggests that entrepreneurs and corporate leaders tend to engage in behavior that reproduces the theories we teach them; in this case, perhaps in the form of self-interested behavior that reinforces the maladies of neoliberalism. How might the world change if corporate leaders were taught strategy in a way that valorizes social relationships and culture, and promotes altruism over self-interest?

These are important questions to ponder because we believe these issues matter. Likewise, we emphasize the importance of ontology because we believe it matters – not only for scholarship and scholarly identity, but for the world we live in. The politics of knowledge is interpenetrated with the politics of the social world and different views about how the world works, as well as what kind of world we want to live in. It seems that students in our programs should be exposed to content that reflects more diverse ontologies which will enable more critical thinking and reflexivity. No single approach should be dominant.

Next, in our concluding chapter, we reprise the main arguments of the book and encourage students and early career researchers to consider how they might become more engaged scholars and study big problems in the world, including so-called grand challenges. We see these as important additional considerations in the cultivation of a scholarly identity. In addition, by discussing the role of organization theorists in addressing grand challenges, we continue to emphasize the broad reach of organization theory. Organization theory is relevant to everything in world, and organization theorists can teach almost anything. This goes well beyond the staples of entrepreneurship and strategy to include courses on business and society, management analytics, leadership, decision-making, negotiations, social innovation, and public policy, just to name a few.

6. Conclusion: building a robust scholarly identity

We began the book by foregrounding the importance of ontological assumptions that distinguish theoretical conversations (and researchers) from each other. Recognizing the diverse theoretical contributions since Burrell and Morgan's (1979) landmark book, we proposed two key ontological dimensions for understanding contemporary organization theory. On one axis, contextual emphasis distinguishes between theories that stress the importance of economic, social, or cultural aspects of an organization's context. The other axis highlights how theories conceptualize actors, distinguishing between exogenous and endogenous understandings of the actor-context relationship. Alongside these ontological differences, we drew attention to the axiological commitments latent in different philosophies of science, as a way of both making them explicit and sparking theoretical imagination about possible alternatives.

Utilizing these resources, we introduced and reviewed three different sets of theoretical packages, explicating their different ontological and axiological commitments. We explored rational choice theories rooted in utilitarianism in Chapter 2. Then, in Chapter 3, we considered pragmatic theories built on American pragmatism. In Chapter 4, we focused on co-constitutive theories informed by phenomenology and continental philosophy. Taking a more panoptic view in Chapter 5, we explored how these three theoretical packages have been differentially refracted within the domains of entrepreneurship and strategy research.

In this chapter, we return to one of the book's other major ambitions: articulating opportunities for emerging scholars to develop robust identities (i.e., identities with the power to meaningfully contribute to multiple academic conversations, while maximizing the potential for real-world relevance across diverse contexts). Indeed, one of our key objectives in writing this book was to spark conversations with emerging scholars who are in the throes of establishing their identities. We see numerous pathways for those who are able to develop multivocal and multiplex insights – theoretical, empirical, and methodological contributions that can speak to multiple audiences inside and outside the academy, audiences whose members are apt to subscribe to their own thought worlds and bring their own values commitments to bear.

For these reasons (and others unpacked below), we believe that college deans and university administrators will increasingly recognize organization scholars as potent and versatile faculty members. For instance, many organization scholars teach in business schools. In 2020, the Association to Advance Collegiate Schools of Business (AACSB) updated the standards guiding its accreditation process. Notably, two new standards were introduced – Standard 8: Impact of Scholarship "focuses on the production, dissemination, and impact of a school's thought leadership as it relates to scholarship," and Standard 9: Engagement and Societal Impact "assesses a school's engagement with and impact on society" (AACSB, 2021: 49). As these standards make clear, scholarly contributions will continue to be paramount, but they also highlight potential opportunities for impact that extend far beyond specific research topics. Indeed, these standards invoke considerations that organization scholars already actively engage. To explore this terrain, we begin by considering the prospects for building a robust identity in the three core domains of a scholar's life: research, teaching, and outreach. Having considered these three, we turn to recent scholarship on grand challenges with an eye to recapitulating the book's major themes: ontology, axiology, and robustness.

6.1   Engaged scholarship and the impact imperative

Organization and management scholars have long been interested in understanding and addressing social problems (Amis et al., 2020; Gabbioneta et al., 2023; Hinings & Greenwood, 2002; Margolis & Walsh, 2003; Selznick, 1996; Stern & Barley, 1996). By the turn of the 21st century, this impulse was evident in research topics such as climate change (Ansari et al., 2013; Augustine et al., 2019; Schüssler et al., 2014), forced and exploitative labor (Bartley, 2007; Crane, 2013; Khan et al., 2007; Locke, 2013), poverty alleviation (Battilana & Dorado, 2010; Cobb et al., 2016; Dorado & Ventresca, 2013; Mair et al., 2012), and sustainability issues more generally (Bansal & Song, 2016; Crilly et al., 2015; Garud & Gehman, 2012).

At the same time, there has been a discernible shift in how organization scholars understand their identities even as they pursue such research. For instance, several scholars have advocated for engaged scholarship (Cummings, 2007; Hoffman, 2021a; Van de Ven, 2007; Van de Ven & Johnson, 2006). According to Van de Ven and Johnson (2006), at its core, such an approach is an exercise in "intellectual arbitrage" – exploiting differences in the kinds of knowledge that scholars and practitioners can contribute as a way of finding solutions to pertinent problems. However, such arbitrage also involves a shift in how scholars understand their relationships with the communities they are studying. In line with the movement we traced from rationalist to pragmatic to co-constitutive theories, engaged scholarship entails a co-production of "knowledge on important questions and issues by testing alternative ideas and different views of a common problem" (Van de Ven & Johnson, 2006: 809). In other words, engaged scholarship anticipates – and perhaps even necessitates – robust scholarly identities.

Importantly, engaged scholarship also is pluralistic in several ways. First, those involved are likely to hold competing views of reality, or in the terms of this book, plural ontologies and axiologies. According to Van de Ven and Johnson (2006), this creates the potential for fundamental conflicts, which, in their view, can be bridged if the research questions being addressed are formulated in ways that catalyze the engagement of relevant participants. Second, an arbitrage strategy calls for a "pluralist methodology" in which "communication across perspectives is a precondition for establishing robust alternative models of a problem" (Van de Ven & Johnson, 2006: 809; see also Azevedo, 2002). Through such communication and coordination, "robust features of reality can be distinguished" (Azevedo, 1997: 191). The overall imagery that emerges is fundamentally meta-theoretical in the sense that multiple explanations are simultaneously held in view (e.g., Allison, 1971; Colomy, 1991; Garud & Gehman, 2012; Ritzer, 1992).

Engaged scholarship also emphasizes the importance of scholarly impact, but leaves open the question of how to assess whether this has been achieved (e.g., see Van de Ven, 2007: 233–236). In this regard, several articles have offered new frameworks for thinking about the relationship between theory and impact. For instance, Hernandez and Haack (2023: 373) equated impact with public policy and the public good: "consistent with the aim of serving the public good, it follows that public policy cannot be value free." They proposed that the relationship between management theory and public policy can be distinguished along two dimensions: performativity and permeability. Based on their experiences, they asserted that most articles assume performativity to be low and permeability to be high, "reflecting a descriptive-instrumental treatment of the management theory-public policy relationship," (Hernandez & Haack, 2023: 376) and called for research that populates the three other cells in their imagined matrix.

Reinecke et al. (2022) took a different tack, arguing that a more nuanced appreciation of the relationship between organization theory and its societal impact is needed. Specifically, they proposed the notion of impactful theory and identified seven distinct pathways for attaining theoretical impact. Nested within their typology are three different ways of conceiving of the relationship between theory and impact. Transfer refers to scholarly theories that are employed, more or less faithfully, in situated practices. Co-creation (which includes engaged scholarship) entails a co-production of theory and impact by academics and practitioners. Finally, performativity sees theories as interventions in the world rather than representations of it (e.g., Callon, 2007; Garud & Gehman, 2016). Although they vary in their specifics, both perspectives embrace a plural conception of the theory-impact relationship, and thus provide important resources for scholars interested in developing a robust identity at this interface.

6.2 "Get me an organization theorist, stat!"

So far, we have concentrated on the ramifications of the variegated organization theory landscape for the scholarly research enterprise, but implications of these dynamics extend well beyond the research that we conduct. There are profound implications for our teaching portfolios and our role in pedagogical innovation, as well as our engagement within the universities where we work. Here, we also highlight an important but often overlooked corollary to the academic freedom scholars have long enjoyed: With academic freedom comes a responsibility to participate in the collegial governance and administration of our home institutions. Robust identities can aid in these endeavors by facilitating efforts to build bridges and foster conversations within and across campuses and disciplines.

Easily overlooked is one of the most valuable parts of the doctoral training we receive as organization scholars – namely, the broad knowledge we acquire, as well as the ability to rapidly update our understanding of particular domains and assimilate entirely new bodies of knowledge. In addition to the depth and breadth of our doctoral training, it is not uncommon for organization scholars to have spent considerable time working as practitioners in organizations before or during our doctoral studies. Viewed in terms of our role as university teachers, this means we have the requisite tools to teach with authenticity and nuance about topics that extend well beyond the specifics of our research.

Although some people are dismissive of the idea that "organization theorists can teach anything," this aphorism captures an essential truth, in part because the phenomena studied by our field span conventional divisions, such as between micro and macro (e.g., Astley & Van de Ven, 1983; Lawrence & Phillips, 2019). For instance, in addition to workhorse courses such as management, strategy, and entrepreneurship, organization scholars regularly teach courses such as business ethics, negotiations, power and politics, leadership, people management, and social networks. Organization theorists also have been at the forefront of introducing courses on ascendent topics such as social entrepreneurship and social innovation, managing corporate sustainability, business analytics, and social movements. More recently, our colleagues have introduced courses on subjects such as equity analytics (Rider et al., 2023), impact investing, lobbying and regulation, remaking capitalism (Henderson, 2020; Marquis, 2020), and even fundamental questions such as the relationship between business and democracy itself.

These developments are consequential, in part because tomorrow's leaders will need much more than knowledge about accounting, finance, and operations management. Looking ahead, we encourage emerging scholars to view the development of a diverse teaching portfolio in general, and the introduction of new courses in particular, as another facet of their robust identities. As businesses, nonprofits, and governments grapple with topics such as digitalization, artificial intelligence, and environmental, social, and corporate governance (ESG) assessment, organization scholars can contribute by staying at the forefront of translating what we know about organizations and organizing in ways that resonate with tomorrow's students – from frontline managers to C-suite executives. For emerging organization scholars, this offers yet another opportunity to embrace a robust identity and find new ways to make meaningful impacts on the world.

In addition to playing a more visible and active role in teaching and pedagogical innovation, we encourage tomorrow's scholars to take a more active role in the governance and administration of their universities. We think it is important to recognize that alongside academic freedom comes the responsibility to take an active role in university governance. Of course, participating in university life has always been important. But considering the many threats now confronting universities – from the encroachment of politics on university decision-making and dramatic reductions in state support for public education, to widespread financialization and the embracement of a corporatist logic throughout the university structure – it is essential that organization scholars take seriously their responsibilities to participate in university governance at all levels. This means getting actively involved in administration, from our home departments (e.g., Crossland, 2023) to school and college level committees and offices, from university senates, committees, and taskforces to central university governance and administration. It is our responsibility to fight for and participate in the collegial governance of our institutions (Sahlin & Eriksson-Zetterquist, 2024).

6.3   The remaking of the public intellectual

Beyond the walls of our classrooms and the borders of our university campuses, robust identities provide academics with a platform for engaging with diverse stakeholders in the public square, an area where management scholars have long advocated for more engagement. For instance, in 1993, the president of the Academy of Management, Don Hambrick, pointedly asked: "What if the Academy actually mattered?" His goal in asking this question was to create "a nagging uneasiness about the gap between what we as an Academy amount to and what we might amount to," in the hopes it would "stir us to raise our sights for the future" (Hambrick, 1994: 13). Looking back over the past three decades, many organization scholars have taken quite seriously the admonition to "matter." At the same time, it is possible to discern a shift in the type of "mattering" that resonates with scholars (e.g., George et al., 2016; Hinings & Greenwood, 2002; Margolis & Walsh, 2003; Reinecke et al., 2022; Stern & Barley, 1996).

To grasp the magnitude of the shift, consider the 2017 Academy of Management presidential address Anita McGahan delivered in Atlanta, Georgia, roughly a quarter-century after Hambrick's. Proposing that "the problems of Atlanta, and of the United States, and of the world, are our problems as management scholars" (McGahan, 2018: 174), she advocated for scholars to "double down even more intently on the management of organizations designed to address the most important problems of our time … because the problems on the street outside and at our borders and in the world around us are our problems" (p. 175). As part of this "doubling down," she specifically advocated that scholars embrace our standing as public intellectuals. Although management academics tend to speak out only when we feel particularly qualified to do so, McGahan (2018: 175) reasoned that scholars should blog, tweet, and speak out about "what you believe to be true based on the results of your research … The world needs science – the construction of facts and the truth – about great management that creates jobs, supports freedom, transforms vulnerabilities into strengths, stops climate change, and creates prosperity for everyone."

We agree with these sentiments on the importance of embracing our role as public intellectuals, and it seems an increasing number of our colleagues feel similarly (e.g., Adler et al., 2007; Hoffman, 2021b). At the same time, we wish to highlight an important implication of this increased public engagement, and to clarify the kind of engagement we have in mind.

First, public engagement, on its own, is unlikely to lead to convergence in knowledge claims or agreement on facts and truth, which we think is what many implicitly have in mind when they advocate for practices such as evidence-based management (e.g., Learmonth, 2008; Reay et al., 2009; Rousseau, 2012). For instance, consider the dynamics that unfolded when scholars became engaged in the debate over hydraulic fracturing, a contentious practice in the oil and gas industry (Etzion & Gehman, 2019). On one side of the fracking debate was Terry Engelder, a professor of geosciences at Pennsylvania State University. Engelder advocated for fracking because of the immense economic boost it could provide to local communities. On the other side of the debate was Anthony Ingraffea, a professor of civil engineering at Cornell University. For Ingraffea, fracking was to be avoided at all costs because of its potentially negative health consequences for local communities and the magnitude of its implications for climate change. Far from generating convergence, debates between Engelder and Ingraffea created dissonance because, in their own ways, both were right: They had "decades of experience and ample peer-reviewed research to back up their claims" (Etzion & Gehman, 2019: 487).

The debate over fracking, as with most social questions, was (and is) values-laden. For management scholars, this means there is not a values-neutral position from which to enter such debates (see also Cornelissen et al., 2021; Hernandez & Haack, 2023). This is another reason why it is so critical to be aware of the axiological commitments undergirding the theoretical approaches we employ. To wit, research can inform questions about more or less effective ways for companies to conduct their hydraulic fracturing operations, but such insights do not speak to questions of whether to engage in such practices in the first place. Moreover, in the case of fracking, each new piece of research, rather than settling disputes, augments the criteria under consideration, multiplying rather than ameliorating contention and controversy. In general, more science often makes controversies worse (Sarewitz, 2004). For scholars committed to engagement in the public square, this means we should expect to encounter plurality, and even cacophony, as our contributions intersect with other voices animated by different values considerations and other lines of evidence.

Our second point flows from these realities. The kind of public engagement we envision is not one of prescription. As public intellectuals, we do not believe it is our place to tell members of society how they should live, but to foster theoretically informed understandings about how lines of action produce certain consequences. Determining whether societies want more or less of certain outcomes requires engaging in political and ethical debates. Our work can inform an understanding of how it could be otherwise. But ultimately, for us, the theoretical gaze is about opening new possibilities, not imposing particular prescriptions or proscriptions. This creates opportunities for scholars at all career stages to experiment with mobilizing what they know about organizations and organizing in ways that capture the attention of managers, policymakers and citizens across the entire range of organizational modes – corporations, nonprofits, and government agencies. Viewed against this backdrop, it seems clear to us that organization theory has never been more relevant to the problems of the day than right now.

6.4 Tackling grand challenges

In addition to the opportunities for developing a robust scholarly identity across one's entire portfolio of research, teaching and outreach, we believe these considerations are even more germane, given the increasing focus among organization scholars on understanding and tackling grand challenges – ranging from persistent problems such as refugee crises, poverty, and inequality to emerging concerns such as climate change, artificial intelligence, and extreme weather. Accordingly, to close out the book, we offer one final illustration. Namely, we consider the burgeoning research on grand challenges through the lens of our framework of ontological differences and the quest for a robust identity. For emerging scholars, this changing topology creates exciting possibilities to bridge different literatures and establish links between different communities.

To start, within the wider scientific community, the concept of "grand challenges" emerged over the past several decades as an umbrella term for encompassing scholarship on a wide array of pressing concerns (for reviews, see Flink & Kaldewey, 2018; Kaldewey, 2018). Initially, the focus was on scientific and technical challenges, but over time, attention shifted to social and cultural challenges. Within the field of management, the topic of grand challenges only gained traction in the early 2010s. This was notably seeded by a journal editorial (Colquitt & George, 2011: 432) asserting that "the fundamental principles underlying a grand challenge are the pursuit of bold ideas and the adoption of less conventional approaches to tackling large, unresolved problems."

Following this initial invocation of the term, the focus on grand challenges gained rapid prominence as a result of a few early publications (e.g., Ferraro et al., 2015; George et al., 2016). There have since been many workshops and consortia themed around the topic of grand challenges, including a string of events at the Academy of Management Annual

Meetings (e.g., Cascadden et al., 2021; Danner-Schröder et al., 2022; Delmestri et al., 2017; Etchanchu et al., 2019), as well as special issues (Howard-Grenville et al., 2019; Voegtlin et al., 2022) and edited volumes (Gehman et al., 2024; Gümüsay et al., 2022) dealing with different facets of grand challenges. Given the explosion in grand challenges research, scholars have aimed to take stock of the burgeoning work in this area in a growing number of literature reviews (e.g., Brammer et al., 2019; Fernhaber & Zou, 2022; Howard-Grenville & Spengler, 2022; Kaufmann & Danner-Schröder, 2022).

Already, several definitions of grand challenges have emerged. In the introduction to the first special issue on the topic, George et al. (2016: 1880, 1881) defined grand challenges as "formulations of global problems that can be plausibly addressed through coordinated and collaborative effort" and, as "specific critical barrier(s) that, if removed, would help solve an important societal problem with a high likelihood of global impact through widespread implementation." Ferraro and colleagues (2015) opted for a more analytical approach, enumerating three facets of grand challenges: complexity, uncertainty, and evaluativity. Building on this framework, they conceptualized grand challenges "as matters of concern that entail complexity, evoke uncertainty, and provoke evaluativity" (Gehman, Etzion, et al., 2022: 260). One of the benefits of this definition is that it anticipates variation in scope (e.g., some concerns may be more global whereas others may be quite local), variation in consensus regarding priority (e.g., some concerns may be widely accepted, whereas others may not be), and variation in the tractability of constraints (e.g., some concerns may be ameliorable via the removal of a common barrier, whereas others may be much less tractable). "Critically, this definition problematizes the possibility of drawing a delimited list of challenges once and for all" (p. 260).

In addressing these topics, organization scholars have increasingly embraced research approaches such as engaged scholarship and other research designs that enable the development of theoretical explanations and contextualized insights with potential for real-world impact (e.g., Bartkus & Block, 2024; Hoffman, 2021a; Kistruck & Slade Shantz, 2022; Reinecke et al., 2022; Van de Ven, 2007; Wry & Haugh, 2018). In taking up these questions and toolkits, it is important for scholars to consider not only their individual positions in the field, but also how they can position their findings and insights in ways that foster uptake by a wide variety of audiences. Against this backdrop, it is interesting to consider research on grand challenges relative to the different ontological positions we have mapped throughout this book.

As we described in Chapter 2, rationalist theories stress the importance of material resources and are rooted in utilitarian philosophy. Germane to the topic of grand challenges, the allure of their assumptions – e.g., that actors are purposive, self-interested and wealth-maximizing – has resulted in the widespread adoption of rational choice-inspired policy interventions. For instance, Vakili and McGahan (2016) examined the impact of the World Trade Organization's (WTO) 1994 Trade-Related Intellectual Property Rights Agreement (TRIPS), which aimed to improve the availability of drugs for "neglected diseases" such as malaria and tuberculosis in low-income countries. Consistent with our exposition of rational choice theories, TRIPS was built on an "economic logic" rooted in the assumption that intellectual property protections, such as patent rights, create incentives without which pharmaceutical companies would not engage in risky and expensive development activities. Consistent with this rational choice logic, the WTO mandated that countries implement intellectual property protections as a condition of membership. Although initially a controversial requirement, ultimately "representatives from low-income countries agreed with the argument that TRIPS would create an incentive in the global pharmaceutical industry for new research on neglected diseases" (Vakili & McGahan, 2016: 1919).

Unfortunately, economists who have studied TRIPS have found little evidence that the availability of patent rights has led to the development of new drugs for neglected diseases, but it has led to the development of drugs for nonneglected diseases. For Vakili and McGahan (2016), this surfaced a puzzle as to why the implementation of patent rights led to the development of new drugs for nonneglected diseases but not for neglected diseases. They proposed two explanations for this asymmetrical effect. First, basic science is a prerequisite for drug development. Second, a "constellation" of managerial actions is required to develop and commercialize drugs for neglected diseases, and these activities may take longer to come to fruition than for nonneglected diseases. Together, they referred to these as "institutions and managerial practices of science." Their analysis shows that economic incentives and self-interest are insufficient to motivate efforts to address health-related grand challenges. A critical ingredient is institutional readiness on the part of scientists to respond to economic incentives, reminiscent of the performative dynamics scholars have highlighted in the context of economics more generally (Callon, 2007; MacKenzie & Millo, 2003).

Going beyond this research, several studies have reported that efforts to tackle grand challenges designed around rational choice assumptions are seldom effective. For instance, in their classic study of industry self-regulation in the chemical industry, King and Lenox (2000) found that firm-level opportunism was more powerful than industry-level isomorphic pressures, leading them to conclude that it is difficult to maintain effective industry self-regulation without explicit sanctions, an explanation consistent with rational choice theories. In a similar vein, Wright and Nyberg (2017: 1633) found that several major corporations "translated" climate change from a revolutionary challenge into "the mundane and comfortable concerns of 'business as usual.'" Once again, their analysis suggests that rational choice considerations are to blame, for instance, owing to a lack of incentives to invest in decarbonization and market pressures favoring continued economic growth.

In their study of soccer ball manufacturers in Sialkot, Pakistan, Khan and colleagues (2007) found that even well-intentioned interventions can have a dark side. Namely, they examined the issue of child labor, which gained global attention in 1995 after CBS broadcast images of children sewing soccer balls in seemingly exploitative conditions. In response, multiple actors sprang into action, including numerous industrial, national, and international bodies (e.g., FIFA, International Confederation of Free Trade Unions, ILO, Sialkot Chamber of Commerce and Industry, UNICEF, US Department of Labor, World Federation Sporting Goods Industry, and so forth). Ultimately, the Sialkot Child Labor Elimination Project was launched. Consistent with rational choice theories and reminiscent of TRIPS, this initiative mandated that sewing move from village homes to so-called stitching centers, which would facilitate monitoring for and sanctioning of child labor. As a result of this intervention, by July 2003, 95% of all soccer ball exports were declared to have been manufactured free of child labor. A variety of leaders, including U.S. President Bill Clinton, hailed the project as a successful example of an industry–civil society collaboration to tackle social problems. However, this "success" was not without its dark sides: "the benefits for children were questionable, and … the majority of women stitchers had to drop out of the workforce, plunging their families into deeper poverty" (Khan et al., 2007: 1056).

For management scholars, it is perhaps not surprising that rational choice theories would struggle to address certain grand challenges. As Jim March (2006: 201) taught us, "technologies of rationality seem clearly to be effective instruments of exploitation in relatively simple situations." In part, this is because such approaches were developed expressly for solving "problems of focused relevance, limited temporal and spatial perspectives, and moderate complexity" (p. 207). But, as a corollary, rationality is not necessarily well-suited to tackling grand challenges, at least to the extent they involve more than moderate complexity, which most scholars consider to be the case.

In view of this circumstance, other management scholars have proposed or employed explicitly managerialist frameworks to inform the relevant considerations for organizations seeking to address grand challenges. For instance, George et al. (2023: 4) enumerated five "managerial problems in organizing for grand challenges;" these include the fact that grand challenges are global, complex, characterized by uncertainty, often consist of "diverging and paradoxical interests," and unfold over extended time scales. According to these authors, even a multiactor public-private collaboration "can be treated as an organization in and of itself;" in turn, "this perspective gives us access to a menu of concepts and tools for understanding … the ways in which the collaboration is constructed to address fundamental problems in the division of responsibilities and in the cultivation of coordinated action aligned with critical goals" (p. 13).

It is here that pragmatic theories, such as those we considered in Chapter 3, may have more to offer. Ferraro and colleagues (2015) proposed a robust action approach to tackling grand challenges, building specifically on American pragmatism, which, in their telling, emphasizes a situated, distributed, and processual approach to problem solving. Building these ontological underpinnings, they revisited the sociological concept of robust action (Leifer, 1991; Padgett & Ansell, 1993), commonly defined as "noncommittal actions that keep future lines of action open in strategic contexts where opponents are trying to narrow them" (Padgett & Powell, 2012: 24), and considered how such an approach might enable organizations to contribute to tackling grand challenges.

Specifically, Ferraro and colleagues (2015: 373) proposed three robust strategies for dealing with grand challenges: participatory architecture, defined as "a structure and rules of engagement that allow diverse and heterogeneous actors to interact constructively over prolonged time-spans;" multivocal inscription, defined as "discursive and material activity that sustains different interpretations among various audiences with different evaluative criteria, in a manner that promotes coordination without requiring explicit consensus;" and distributed experimentation, defined as "iterative action that generates small wins, promotes evolutionary learning and increases engagement, while allowing unsuccessful efforts to be abandoned." Their initial statement drew on extant research to illustrate these strategies with examples related to the Global Reporting Initiative, the United Nations Principles for Responsible Investing and the Forestry Stewardship Council.

Recently, Porter and colleagues (2020) focused on one of the potential shortcomings of robust action: the time it takes to generate scalable impact. In this regard, they argued that crowdsourcing – an approach that organizations have begun using to stimulate collaborative problem-solving on a range of societal issues – could be a valuable tool for achieving scalable impact. Through their in-depth study of Save Our Oceans, an initiative aimed at developing sustainability related innovation in the maritime industry, Porter and colleagues (2020: 248) found that robust action strategies were instrumental in "generating novel ideas, attracting the participation of diverse stakeholder groups, and building a network of resources to further develop novel ideas into sustainable solutions." But, they also found that momentum and novelty generation were precarious accomplishments, at risk of getting lost in the shuffle as actors came and went. Here, they uncovered a second benefit of a pragmatism: By deploying robust action strategies, the organization they studied was able to build connections between ideas and actors across crowdfunding phases, thereby achieving more scalable impact.

This brings us to phenomenology and the co-constitutive theories we introduced in Chapter 4. As we have seen, such theories problematize conventional understandings of actors, and instead emphasize how agentic possibilities are themselves shaped by the ongoing and historical interplay with wider cultural processes (Douglas, 1970; Meyer, 2010; Ruef, 1999). From this perspective, actorhood is neither pregiven nor fixed; new kinds of actors can emerge, older ones may disappear, and capacities may expand or contract (Fligstein & McAdam, 2012; Hirschman & Reed, 2014; Lounsbury & Wang, 2020). But what might such sensibilities portend for the study of grand challenges?

One effort in this direction is the concept of institutional entrepreneuring – defined as "the processes whereby actors are created and equipped for action within particular spheres" (Gehman, Sharma, et al., 2022: 290). Building on assemblage theory (Deleuze & Guattari, 1987), these authors heeded calls to move beyond either/or ontological positions (Lounsbury, 2008; Meyer & Vaara, 2020; Smets et al., 2017). Applied to the domain of grand challenges, this approach foregrounds different modes of actorhood, ranging from arborescent to rhizomatic. The former position, arborescent assembling, resonates with rational choice theories. For instance, this ideal-type is committed to hierarchy, homogeneity and dualisms, hews to taken-for-granted concepts, and spreads by means of genealogy and imitation. The latter position, rhizomatic assembling, pushes the frontiers of co-constitutive theories. For instance, in botany, a rhizome is a type of plant that grows horizontally underground and is composed of multiple nodes, any of which can sprout. While these shoots become visible, the rhizome itself remains hidden, as is the case with ferns, spider plants, and bamboo, as well as numerous invasive plants. Taking this imagery as inspiration, rhizomatic assembling emphasizes multiplicity and connections between heterogeneous entities, thereby allowing novel concepts to surface while populating by means of contagion and epidemics.

Mair and Hehenberger's (2014) examination of the emergence of venture philanthropy illustrates some of these ideas. For instance, in place of traditional grantmaking, venture philanthropy sought to foster accountability by establishing terms of reciprocity between funders and recipients. In contrast with the hierarchical and status-driven dynamics typical of elite philanthropy organizations, a mixture of front stage and back stage events facilitated connections between diverse participants in ways that cut across silos, further facilitating the translation and adoption of venture philanthropy models. At the same time, traditional approaches to philanthropy continued to exist in a "mutualistic relationship" (Mair & Hehenberger, 2014: 1188). Another important contribution of the backstage workshops that emerged was their ability to provide relational spaces free from specific constraints, thereby enabling actors to understand and adopt in a more a la carte or ad hoc fashion the venture philanthropy practices that suited their circumstances.

Although research on grand challenges is, in many respects, still in its infancy, in much the same way that scholarship on entrepreneurship and strategic management illustrates and reiterates the ontological contours mapped in the book, we can see evidence of the impulse towards explanations rooted in rational choice theories, pragmatism, and co-constitutive theories. For us, these developments are exciting because they present opportunities to scholars – not only to contribute knowledge about grand challenges, but also to stake out robust identities for themselves in the process.

6.5   Conclusion

In this book, we have sought to provide a broad overview of the organization theory field that helps early career scholars understand its diversity and importance. We foregrounded the role of ontology – assumptions we make about the nature of reality – as crucially important to understanding different theoretical conversations in the field, as well as the complexities associated with cultivating a robust scholarly identity. We also noted how issues related to value and valuing – axiology – are woven into ontological commitments. Given our emphasis on ontological differences, we highlighted three broad classes of theory – rationalist, pragmatic, and co-constitutive – which are undergirded by different philosophical traditions – utilitarianism, American pragmatism, and phenomenology. While exhibiting significant variation within and across broad categories, these ideal types provide useful analytical distinctions that shape different forms of scholarship and scholarly identities.

We argue that these ontological distinctions, rooted in different philosophical assumptions, are consequential not only for scholarship, but also for teaching and outreach. We urge all scholars to mindfully reflect on the importance of such ontological distinctions, and to make informed choices about what kinds of research to pursue and which scholarly identities to cultivate. In addition, we encourage early career organization theorists to consider the value of engaged scholarship and to study big problems in the world – a focus on grand challenges seems particularly opportune to us. In closing, given our fervent belief that organization theory is one of the most vibrant scholarly domains in the field of management, we sincerely hope this book provides a useful roadmap for understanding its richness and diversity, and for navigating one's scholarly journey.

References

AACSB. 2021, July 1. *2020 guiding principles and standards for AACSB business accreditation.* AACSB International. https://www.aacsb.edu/-/media/documents/accreditation/2020-aacsb-business-accreditation-standards-july-2021.pdf.

Abbott, A. 1988. *The system of professions: An essay on the division of expert labor.* Chicago: University of Chicago Press.

Acs, Z. J., & Audretsch, D. B. 1990. *Innovation and small firms.* Cambridge, MA: MIT Press.

Adler, P. S. (Ed.). 2009. *The Oxford handbook of sociology and organization studies: Classical foundations.* Oxford, UK: Oxford University Press.

Adler, P. S., Forbes, L. C., & Willmott, H. 2007. Critical management studies. *Academy of Management Annals,* 1: 119–179.

Aiken, M., & Hage, J. 1968. Organizational interdependence and intra-organizational structure. *American Sociological Review,* 33: 912–930.

Aldrich, H. E. 1979. *Organizations and environments.* Upper Saddle River, NJ: Prentice Hall.

Aldrich, H. E. 2014, November 28. Stand up and be counted: Why social science should stop using the qualitative/quantitative dichotomy. *LSE Impact Blog.* https://blogs.lse.ac.uk/impactofsocialsciences/2014/11/28/stand-up-and-be-counted-social-science-qualitative-quantitative-dichotomy/.

Aldrich, H. E., & Ruef, M. 2006. *Organizations evolving* (2nd ed.). Thousand Oaks, CA: Sage.

Aldrich, H. E., Ruef, M., & Lippmann, S. 2020. *Organizations evolving* (3rd ed.). Northampton, MA: Elgar.

Aldrich, H. E., & Whetten, D. A. 1981. Organization-sets, action-sets, and networks: Making the most of simplicity. In P. C. Nystrom & W. H. Starbuck (Eds.), *Handbook of organizational design: Adapting organizations to their environments,* vol. 1: 385–408. New York: Oxford University Press.

Aldrich, H. E., & Wiedenmayer, G. 1993. From traits to rates: An ecological perspective on organizational foundings. *Advances in Entrepreneurship, Firm Emergence, and Growth,* 1: 145–195.

Aldrich, H. E., & Zimmer, C. 1986. Entrepreneurship through social networks. In D. L. Sexton & R. W. Smilor (Eds.), *The art and science of entrepreneurship*: 3–23. Cambridge, MA: Ballinger.

Allison, G. T. 1971. *Essence of decision: Explaining the Cuban Missile Crisis.* Boston, MA: Little, Brown & Co.

Almandoz, J. 2012. Arriving at the starting line: The impact of community and financial logics on new banking ventures. *Academy of Management Journal*, 55: 1381–1406.

Amis, J. M., Mair, J., & Munir, K. A. 2020. The organizational reproduction of inequality. *Academy of Management Annals*, 14: 195–230.

Anand, N., & Peterson, R. A. 2000. When market information constitutes fields: Sensemaking of markets in the commercial music industry. *Organization Science*, 11: 270–284.

Andrews, K. R. 1971. *The concept of corporate strategy.* Homewood, IL: Dow Jones.

Ansari, S., Wijen, F., & Gray, B. 2013. Constructing a climate change logic: An institutional perspective on the "tragedy of the commons." *Organization Science*, 24: 1014–1040.

Ansell, C. 2009. Mary Parker Follett and pragmatist organization. In P. Adler (Ed.), *The Oxford handbook of sociology and organization studies: Classical foundations*: 464–485. New York: Oxford University Press.

Ansell, C. 2011. *Pragmatist democracy: Evolutionary learning as public philosophy.* New York: Oxford University Press.

Anteby, M., Chan, C. K., & DiBenigno, J. 2016. Three lenses on occupations and professions in organizations: Becoming, doing, and relating. *Academy of Management Annals*, 10: 183–244.

Arrow, K. J. 1983. Innovation in large and small firms. In J. Ronen (Ed.), *Entrepreneurship*: 15–28. Lexington, MA: Lexington Books.

Astley, W. G. 1985. Administrative science as socially constructed truth. *Administrative Science Quarterly*, 30: 497–513.

Astley, W. G., & Van de Ven, A. H. 1983. Central perspectives and debates in organization theory. *Administrative Science Quarterly*, 28: 245–273.

Audia, P. G., & Greve, H. R. 2021. *Organizational learning from performance feedback: A behavioral perspective on multiple goals.* New York: Cambridge University Press.

Audretsch, D. B. 1995. *Innovation and industry evolution.* Cambridge, MA: MIT Press.

Augustine, G. 2021. We're not like those crazy hippies: The dynamics of jurisdictional drift in externally mandated occupational groups. *Organization Science*, 32: 1056–1078.

Augustine, G., Soderstrom, S., Milner, D., & Weber, K. 2019. Constructing a distant future: Imaginaries in geoengineering. *Academy of Management Journal*, 62: 1930–1960.

Austin, J. L. 1962. *How to do things with words.* Oxford, UK: Clarendon Press.

Azevedo, J. 1997. *Mapping reality: An evolutionary realist methodology for the natural social sciences.* Albany, NY: SUNY Press.

Azevedo, J. 2002. Updating organizational epistemology. In J. A. C. Baum (Ed.), *The Blackwell companion to organizations*: 713–732. Malden, MA: Blackwell.

Bacq, S., Hertel, C., & Lumpkin, G. T. 2022. Communities at the nexus of entrepreneurship and societal impact: A cross-disciplinary literature review. *Journal of Business Venturing*, 37(5): 106231.

Bain, J. S. 1956. *Barriers to new competition: Their character and consequences in manufacturing.* Cambridge, MA: Harvard University Press.

Bain, J. S. 1968. *Industrial organization* (2nd ed.). New York: Wiley.
Balogun, J. 2003. From blaming the middle to harnessing its potential: Creating change intermediaries. *British Journal of Management*, 14: 69–83.
Banerjee, S. B. 2022. Decolonizing management theory: A critical perspective. *Journal of Management Studies*, 59: 1074–1087.
Bansal, P., & Song, H.-C. 2016. Similar but not the same: Differentiating corporate sustainability from corporate responsibility. *Academy of Management Annals*, 11: 105–149.
Barley, S. R. 1986. Technology as an occasion for structuring: Evidence from observations of CT scanners and the social order of radiology departments. *Administrative Science Quarterly*, 31: 78–108.
Barley, S. R. 2008. Coalface institutionalism. In R. Greenwood, C. Oliver, R. Suddaby, & K. Sahlin (Eds.), *The Sage handbook of organizational institutionalism*: 490–515. Thousand Oaks, CA: Sage.
Barnard, C. I. 1938. *The functions of the executive*. Cambridge, MA: Harvard University Press.
Barney, J. 1991. Firm resources and sustained competitive advantage. *Journal of Management*, 17: 99–120.
Bartkus, V. O., & Block, E. S. 2024. *Business on the edge: How to turn a profit and improve the lives in the world's toughest places*. New York: Basic Books.
Bartley, T. 2007. Institutional emergence in an era of globalization: The rise of transnational private regulation of labor and environmental conditions. *American Journal of Sociology*, 113: 297–351.
Bastien, F., Coraiola, D. M., & Foster, W. M. 2023. Indigenous peoples and organization studies. *Organization Studies*, 44: 659–675.
Battilana, J., & Casciaro, T. 2021. *Power, for all: How it really works and why it's everyone's business*. New York: Simon & Schuster.
Battilana, J., & Dorado, S. 2010. Building sustainable hybrid organizations: The case of commercial microfinance organizations. *Academy of Management Journal*, 53: 1419–1440.
Battilana, J., Leca, B., & Boxenbaum, E. 2009. How actors change institutions: Towards a theory of institutional entrepreneurship. *Academy of Management Annals*, 3: 65–107.
Battilana, J., & Lee, M. 2014. Advancing research on hybrid organizing: Insights from the study of social enterprises. *Academy of Management Annals*, 8: 397–441.
Baum, J. A. C., Calabrese, T., & Silverman, B. S. 2000. Don't go it alone: Alliance network composition and startups' performance in Canadian biotechnology. *Strategic Management Journal*, 21: 267–294.
Baum, J. A. C., & Powell, W. W. 1995. Cultivating an institutional ecology of organizations: Comment on Hannan, Carroll, Dundon, and Torres. *American Sociological Review*, 60: 529–538.
Baum, J. A. C., & Singh, J. V. (Eds.). 1994. *Evolutionary dynamics of organizations*. New York: Oxford University Press.
Becker, G. S. 1976. *The economic approach to human behavior*. Chicago: University of Chicago Press.
Becker, H. S. 1963. *Outsiders: Studies in the sociology of deviance*. New York: Free Press.

Beckman, C. M. (Ed.). 2021. *Carnegie goes to California: Advancing and celebrating the work of James G. March*. Bingley, UK: Emerald.

Beckman, C. M., & Haunschild, P. R. 2002. Network learning: The effects of partners' heterogeneity of experience on corporate acquisitions. *Administrative Science Quarterly*, 47: 92–124.

Bednarek, R., & Smith, W. K. 2023. "What may be": Inspiration from Mary Parker Follett for paradox theory. *Strategic Organization*, 14761270231151734.

Bendix, R. 1956. *Work and authority in industry: Ideologies of management in the course of industrialization*. New York: John Wiley & Sons.

Bentham, J. 1789. *An introduction to the principles of morals and legislation*. London: T. Payne and Son.

Berger, P. L., & Kellner, H. 1984. *Für eine neue soziologie: Ein essay über methode und profession*. Frankfurt am Main: Fischer-Wissenschaft.

Berger, P. L., & Luckmann, T. 1967. *The social construction of reality*. Garden City, NY: Anchor.

Besanko, D., Dranove, D., Shanley, M., & Schaefer, M. 2015. *Economics of strategy* (7th ed.). New York: Wiley.

Besharov, M. L., & Smith, W. K. 2014. Multiple institutional logics in organizations: Explaining their varied nature and implications. *Academy of Management Review*, 39: 364–381.

Besharov, M., & Mitzinneck, B. (Eds.). 2020. *Organizational hybridity: Perspectives, processes, promises. Research in the sociology of organizations*, vol. 69. Bingley, UK: Emerald.

Beunza, D., & Ferraro, F. 2019. Performative work: Bridging performativity and institutional theory in the responsible investment field. *Organization Studies*, 40: 515–543.

Beyer, C. 2018. Edmund Husserl. In E. N. Zalta (Ed.), *The Stanford encyclopedia of philosophy* (Summer 2018). Stanford, CA: Stanford University. https://plato.stanford.edu/archives/sum2018/entries/husserl/.

Bidwell, M., & Briscoe, F. 2010. The dynamics of interorganizational careers. *Organization Science*, 21: 1034–1053.

Blau, P. M., & Scott, W. R. 1962. *Formal organizations: A comparative approach*. San Francisco: Chandler Publications.

Bourdieu, P. 1977. *Outline of a theory of practice*. Cambridge, UK: Cambridge University Press.

Bourdieu, P. 1990. *The logic of practice*. Stanford, CA: Stanford University Press.

Brammer, S., Branicki, L., Linnenluecke, M., & Smith, T. 2019. Grand challenges in management research: Attributes, achievements, and advancement. *Australian Journal of Management*, 44: 517–533.

Brass, D. J. 2022. New developments in social network analysis. *Annual Review of Organizational Psychology and Organizational Behavior*, 9: 225–246.

Brass, D. J., & Borgatti, S. P. 2020. *Social networks at work*. London: Routledge.

Brewer, M. B. 1991. The social self: On being the same and different at the same time. *Personality and Social Psychology Bulletin*, 17: 475–482.

Briscoe, F., & Gupta, A. 2016. Social activism in and around organizations. *Academy of Management Annals*, 10: 671–727.

Briscoe, F., King, B., & Leitzinger, J. 2018. *Social movements, stakeholders and non-market strategy*. Bingley, UK: Emerald.

Briscoe, F., & Safford, S. 2008. The Nixon-in-China effect: Activism, imitation and the institutionalization of contentious practices. *Administrative Science Quarterly*, 53: 460–491.

Bromley, P., & Meyer, J. W. 2015. *Hyper-organization: Global organizational expansion*. Oxford, UK: Oxford University Press.

Bromley, P., Meyer, J. W., & Jia, R. 2022. Entrepreneurship as cultural theme in neoliberal society. In R. N. Eberhart, M. Lounsbury, & H. E. Aldrich (Eds.), *Entrepreneurialism and society: New theoretical perspectives. Research in the sociology of organizations*, vol. 81: 55–75. Bingley, UK: Emerald.

Brown, A. D., & Humphreys, M. 2003. Epic and tragic tales: Making sense of change. *Journal of Applied Behavioral Science*, 39: 121–144.

Buchter, L. 2021. Escaping the ellipsis of diversity: Insider activists' use of implementation resources to influence organization policy. *Administrative Science Quarterly*, 66: 521–565.

Burns, T., & Stalker, G. M. 1961. *The management of innovation*. London: Tavistock.

Burrell, G., & Morgan, G. 1979. *Sociological paradigms and organizational analysis*. Portsmouth, NH: Heineman.

Burt, R. S. 1982. *Toward a structural theory of action: Network models of social structure, perception and action*. New York: Academic Press.

Burt, R. S. 1992. *Structural holes: The social structure of competition*. Cambridge, MA: Harvard University Press.

Burt, R. S. 2004. Structural holes and good ideas. *American Journal of Sociology*, 110: 349–399.

Butler, J. 1988. Performative acts and gender constitution: An essay in phenomenology and feminist theory. *Theatre Journal*, 40: 519–531.

Butler, J. 1993. *Bodies that matter: On the discursive limits of sex*. London: Taylor & Francis.

Butler, J. 1997. *Excitable speech: A politics of the performative*. London: Routledge.

Callon, M. 1986. Some elements of a sociology of translation: Domestication of the scallops and the fishermen of St. Brieuc bay. In J. Law (Ed.), *Power, action and belief*: 196–233. Boston: Routledge & Kegan Paul.

Callon, M. 1998a. Introduction: The embeddedness of economic markets in economics. *The Sociological Review*, 46: 1–57.

Callon, M. (Ed.). 1998b. *The laws of the markets*. Malden, MA: Blackwell.

Callon, M. 2007. What does it mean to say that economics is performative? In D. A. MacKenzie, F. Muniesa, & L. Siu (Eds.), *Do economists make markets? On the performativity of economics*: 311–357. Princeton, NJ: Princeton University Press.

Callon, M. 2021. *Markets in the making: Rethinking competition, goods, and innovation*. Princeton, NJ: Princeton University Press.

Cappellaro, G., Tracey, P., & Greenwood, R. 2020. From logic acceptance to logic rejection: The process of destabilization in hybrid organizations. *Organization Science*, 31: 415–438.

Carroll, G. R., & Hannan, M. T. 2000. *The demography of corporations and industries*. Princeton, NJ: Princeton University Press.

Carton, G. 2020. How assemblages change when theories become performative: The case of the blue ocean strategy. *Organization Studies*, 41: 1417–1439.

Carton, G., Parigot, J., & Roulet, T. 2023. How not to turn the grand challenges literature into a Tower of Babel? *Business & Society*, 00076503231159385.

Cascadden, M., Etchanchu, H., Lefsrud, L., Munir, K. A., Davis, G. F., et al. 2021. Addressing grand challenges in organization theory: System change through theory, engagement & action. *Academy of Management Proceedings*, 2021: 13911.

Casciaro, T., & Piskorski, M. J. 2005. Power imbalance, mutual dependence, and constraint absorption: A closer look at resource dependence theory. *Administrative Science Quarterly*, 50: 167–199.

Chia, R., & Rasche, A. 2010. Epistemological alternatives for researching strategy as practice: Building and dwelling worldviews. In D. Golsorkhi, L. Rouleau, D. Seidl, & E. Vaara (Eds.), *Cambridge handbook of strategy as practice*: 34–46. New York: Cambridge University Press.

Child, J. 1972. Organization structure and strategies of control: A replication of the Aston study. *Administrative Science Quarterly*, 17: 163–177.

Clegg, S. 1989. *Frameworks of power*. Newbury Park, CA: Sage.

Clegg, S. R., Courpasson, D., & Phillips, N. 2006. *Power and organizations*. Thousand Oaks, CA: Sage.

Clemens, E. S. 1993. Organizational repertoires and institutional change: Women's groups and the transformation of U.S. politics, 1890–1920. *American Journal of Sociology*, 98: 755–798.

Clemens, E. S. 1997. *The people's lobby: Organizational innovation and the rise of interest group politics in the United States, 1890–1925*. Chicago: University of Chicago Press.

Coase, R. H. 1937. The nature of the firm. *Economica*, 4: 386–405.

Coase, R. H. 1960. The problem of social cost. *Journal of Law and Economics*, 3: 1–44.

Cobb, J. A., Wry, T., & Zhao, E. Y. 2016. Funding financial inclusion: Institutional logics and the contextual contingency of funding for microfinance organizations. *Academy of Management Journal*, 59: 2103–2131.

Cohen, W., & Levinthal, D. 1990. Absorptive capacity: A new perspective on learning and innovation. *Administrative Science Quarterly*, 35: 128–152.

Colomy, P. 1991. Metatheorizing in a postpositivist frame. *Sociological Perspectives*, 34: 269–286.

Colquitt, J. A., & George, G. 2011. Publishing in AMJ – Part 1: Topic choice. *Academy of Management Journal*, 54: 432–435.

Cooley, C. H. 1902. *Human nature and the social order*. New York: Scribner's.

Cornelissen, J., Höllerer, M. A., & Seidl, D. 2021. What theory is and can be: Forms of theorizing in organizational scholarship. *Organization Theory*, 2: 26317877211020328.

Cornelissen, J. P. 2012. Sensemaking under pressure: The influence of professional roles and social accountability on the creation of sense. *Organization Science*, 23: 118–137.

Craig, M. P. A., Stevenson, H., & Meadowcroft, J. 2019. Debating nature's value: Epistemic strategy and struggle in the story of 'ecosystem services.' *Journal of Environmental Policy & Planning*, 21: 811–825.

Crane, A. 2013. Modern slavery as a management practice: Exploring the conditions and capabilities for human exploitation. *Academy of Management Review*, 38: 49–69.

Creed, W. E. D., Hudson, B. A., Okhuysen, G. A., & Smith-Crowe, K. 2022. A place in the world: Vulnerability, well-being, and the ubiquitous evaluation that animates participation in institutional processes. *Academy of Management Review*, 47: 358–381.

Creed, W. E. D., & Scully, M. A. 2000. Songs of ourselves: Employees' deployment of social identity in workplace encounters. *Journal of Management Inquiry*, 9: 391–412.

Crilly, D., Hansen, M., & Zollo, M. 2015. The grammar of decoupling: A cognitive-linguistic perspective on firms' sustainability claims and stakeholders' interpretation. *Academy of Management Journal*, 59: 705–729.

Crossland, C. 2023. Letter to a newly invited department chair. *Journal of Management Inquiry*, 32: 243–247.

Cummings, T. G. 2007. Quest for an engaged academy. *Academy of Management Review*, 32: 355–360.

Cuypers, I. R. P., Hennart, J.-F., Silverman, B. S., & Ertug, G. 2021. Transaction cost theory: Past progress, current challenges, and suggestions for the future. *Academy of Management Annals*, 15: 111–150.

Cyert, R. M., & March, J. G. 1963. *A behavioral theory of the firm*. Englewood Cliffs, NJ: Prentice-Hall.

Czarniawska, B., & Hernes, T. (Eds.). 2005. *Actor-network theory and organizing*. Copenhagen: Copenhagen Business School Press.

Czarniawska, B., & Joerges, B. 1996. Travels of ideas. In B. Czarniawska & G. Sevón (Eds.), *Translating organizational change*: 13–48. New York: de Gruyter.

Dacin, M. T., Dacin, P. A., & Tracey, P. 2011. Social entrepreneurship: A critique and future directions. *Organization Science*, 22: 1203–1213.

D'Adderio, L. 2008. The performativity of routines: Theorising the influence of artefacts and distributed agencies on routines dynamics. *Research Policy*, 37: 769–789.

Daft, R. L., & Weick, K. E. 1984. Toward a model of organizations as interpretation systems. *Academy of Management Review*, 9: 284–295.

Dalpiaz, E., Rindova, V., & Ravasi, D. 2016. Combining logics to transform organizational agency blending industry and art at Alessi. *Administrative Science Quarterly*, 61: 347–392.

Danner-Schröder, A., Mahringer, C. A., Sele, K., Gehman, J., Sutcliffe, K. M., et al. 2022. Practice perspectives on grand challenges: Insights from SAP and routine dynamics research. *Academy of Management Proceedings*, 2022: 12536.

Davis, G. F., & McAdam, D. 2000. Corporations, classes, and social movements after managerialism. *Research in Organizational Behavior*, 22: 193–236.

Davis, G. F., McAdam, D., Scott, W. R., & Zald, M. N. (Eds.). 2005. *Social movements and organization theory*. Cambridge, UK: Cambridge University Press.

Davis, G. F., & Thompson, T. A. 1994. A social movement perspective on corporate control. *Administrative Science Quarterly*, 39: 141–173.

Davis, M. S. 1971. That's interesting! Towards a phenomenology of sociology and a sociology of phenomenology. *Philosophy of the Social Sciences*, 1: 309–344.

de Bakker, F. G. A., den Hond, F., King, B., & Weber, K. 2013. Social movements, civil society and corporations: Taking stock and looking ahead. *Organization Studies*, 34: 573–593.

De Monticelli, R. 2020. The phenomenology of rational agency. In C. Erhard & T. Keiling (Eds.), *The Routledge handbook of phenomenology of agency*: 362–375. New York: Routledge.

de Vaujany, F.-X., Aroles, J., & Pérezts, M. (Eds.). 2023a. *The Oxford handbook of phenomenologies and organization studies*. New York: Oxford University Press.

de Vaujany, F.-X., Aroles, J., & Pérezts, M. 2023b. Phenomenologies and organization studies: Organizing through and beyond appearances. In F.-X. de Vaujany, J. Aroles, & M. Pérezts (Eds.), *The Oxford handbook of phenomenologies and organization studies*: 1–24. New York: Oxford University Press.

Deephouse, D. L. 1999. To be different, or to be the same? It's a question (and theory) of strategic balance. *Strategic Management Journal*, 20: 147–166.

Deephouse, D. L., & Suchman, M. 2008. Legitimacy in organizational institutionalism. In R. Greenwood, C. Oliver, R. Suddaby, & K. Sahlin-Andersson (Eds.), *The Sage handbook of organizational institutionalism*: 49–77. Thousand Oaks, CA: Sage.

DeJordy, R., Scully, M., Ventresca, M. J., & Creed, W. E. D. 2020. Inhabited ecosystems: Propelling transformative social change between and through organizations. *Administrative Science Quarterly*, 65: 931–971.

DeLanda, M. 2009. Ecology and realist ontology. In B. Herzogenrath (Ed.), *Deleuze/Guattari & ecology*: 23–41. New York: Palgrave Macmillan.

Delbridge, R., & Fiss, P. C. 2013. Styles of theorizing and the social organization of knowledge. *Academy of Management Review*, 38: 325–331.

Deleuze, G., & Guattari, F. 1987. *A thousand plateaus: Capitalism and schizophrenia*. (B. Massumi, Tran.). Minneapolis, MN: University of Minnesota Press.

Delmestri, G., Goodrick, E., Ueberbacher, F., Greenwood, R., Scherer, A. G., et al. 2017. Addressing grand challenges with institutional research: The critical role of power. *Academy of Management Proceedings*, 2017: 13692.

Dewey, J. 1933. *How we think*. Boston: Heath & Co.

Dewey, J. 1960. *Theory of the moral life*. New York: Holt, Rinehart and Winston.

DiMaggio, P. 1982. Cultural entrepreneurship in nineteenth-century Boston: The creation of an organizational base for high culture in America. *Media, Culture & Society*, 4: 33–50.

DiMaggio, P. 1986. *Nonprofit enterprise in the arts: Studies in mission and constraint*. Oxford, UK: Oxford University Press.

DiMaggio, P. J. 1988. Interest and agency in institutional theory. In L. G. Zucker (Ed.), *Institutional patterns and organizations: Culture and environment*: 3–21. Cambridge, MA: Ballinger.

DiMaggio, P. J., & Powell, W. W. 1983. The iron cage revisited: Institutional isomorphism and collective rationality in organizational fields. *American Sociological Review*, 48: 147–160.

DiMaggio, P. J., & Powell, W. W. 1991. Introduction. In W. W. Powell & P. J. DiMaggio (Eds.), *The new institutionalism in organizational analysis*: 1–38. Chicago: University of Chicago Press.

Dittrich, K., Guérard, S., & Seidl, D. 2016. Talking about routines: The role of reflective talk in routine change. *Organization Science*, 27: 678–697.

Dobbin, F. 2009. *Inventing equal opportunity*. Princeton, NJ: Princeton University Press.

Dobbin, F. R. 1992. The origins of private social insurance: Public policy and fringe benefits in America, 1920-1950. *American Journal of Sociology*, 97: 1416-1450.

Dobbin, F., Sutton, J. R., Meyer, J. W., & Scott, R. 1993. Equal opportunity law and the construction of internal labor markets. *American Journal of Sociology*, 99: 396-427.

Donaldson, L. 2005. Organization theory as a positive science. In C. Knudsen & H. Tsoukas (Eds.), *The Oxford handbook of organization theory*: 39-62. New York: Oxford University Press.

Donaldson, L., & Luo, B. N. 2014. The Aston Programme contribution to organizational research: A literature review. *International Journal of Management Reviews*, 16: 84-104.

Dorado, S., & Ventresca, M. J. 2013. Crescive entrepreneurship in complex social problems: Institutional conditions for entrepreneurial engagement. *Journal of Business Venturing*, 28: 69-82.

Dosi, G., & Marengo, L. 1994. Some elements of an evolutionary theory of organizational competences. In R. W. England (Ed.), *Evolutionary concepts in contemporary economics*: 157-178. Ann Arbor, MI: University of Michigan Press.

Dosi, G., Nelson, R., & Winter, S. 2000. *The nature and dynamics of organizational capabilities*. New York: Oxford University Press.

Doty, D. H., & Glick, W. H. 1994. Typologies as a unique form of theory building: Toward improved understanding and modeling. *Academy of Management Review*, 19: 230-251.

Doucette, M. B., Gladstone, J. S., & Carter, T. 2021. Indigenous conversational approach to history and business education. *Academy of Management Learning & Education*, 20: 473-484.

Dougherty, D. 1992. Interpretative barriers to successful product innovation in large firms. *Organization Science*, 3: 179-202.

Douglas, M. 1970. *Natural symbols: Explorations in cosmology*. New York: Pantheon Books.

Dreyfus, H. L. 2014. *Skillful coping*. (M. A. Wrathall, Ed.). New York: Oxford University Press.

Dreyfus, H. L., & Dreyfus, S. E. 1984. From Socrates to expert systems: The limits of calculative rationality. *Technology in Society*, 6: 217-233.

Driver, J. 2022. The history of utilitarianism. In E. N. Zalta & U. Nodelman (Eds.), *The Stanford encyclopedia of philosophy* (Winter 2022). Metaphysics Research Lab, Stanford University. https://plato.stanford.edu/archives/win2022/entries/utilitarianism-history/.

Duncan, R. B. 1972. Characteristics of organizational environments and perceived environmental uncertainty. *Administrative Science Quarterly*, 17: 313-327.

Dunn, M. B., & Jones, C. 2010. Institutional logics and institutional pluralism: The contestation of care and science logics in medical education, 1967-2005. *Administrative Science Quarterly*, 55: 114-149.

Durand, R., & Calori, R. 2006. Sameness, otherness? Enriching organizational change theories with philosophical considerations on the same and the other. *Academy of Management Review*, 31: 93-114.

Eberhart, R. N., Lounsbury, M., & Aldrich, H. E. (Eds.). 2022a. *Entrepreneurialism and society: New theoretical perspectives. Research in the sociology of organizations*, vol 81. Bingley, UK: Emerald.

Eberhart, R. N., Lounsbury, M., & Aldrich, H. E. (Eds.). 2022b. *Entrepreneurialism and society: Consequences and meanings. Research in the sociology of organizations*, vol. 82. Bingley, UK: Emerald.

Eisenhardt, K. M. 1989. Agency theory: An assessment and review. *Academy of Management Review*, 14: 57–74.

Eisenhardt, K. M., & Bourgeois, L. J. 1988. Politics of strategic decision making in high-velocity environments: Toward a midrange theory. *Academy of Management Journal*, 31: 737–770.

Eisenhardt, K. M., & Martin, J. A. 2000. Dynamic capabilities: What are they? *Strategic Management Journal*, 21: 1105–1121.

Eisenstadt, S. N. 1980. Cultural orientations, institutional entrepreneurs, and social change: Comparative analysis of traditional civilizations. *American Journal of Sociology*, 85: 840–869.

Elster, J. 2001. Rational choice theory: Cultural concerns. In N. J. Smelser & P. B. Baltes (Eds.), *International encyclopedia of the social & behavioral sciences*: 12763–12768. Oxford, UK: Pergamon.

Emerson, R. M. 1962. Power-dependence relations. *American Sociological Review*, 27: 31–41.

Emery, F. E., & Trist, E. L. 1965. The causal texture of organizational environments. *Human Relations*, 18: 21–32.

Emirbayer, M. 1997. Manifesto for a relational sociology. *American Journal of Sociology*, 103: 281–317.

Emirbayer, M., & Mische, A. 1998. What is agency? *American Journal of Sociology*, 103: 962–1023.

Etchanchu, H., Riaz, M. S., Howard-Grenville, J., Davis, G. F., Gehman, J., et al. 2019. Taking on the challenge: How organization theorists can address grand challenges. *Academy of Management Proceedings*, 2019: 16455.

Etzion, D., & Gehman, J. 2019. Going public: Debating matters of concern as an imperative for management scholars. *Academy of Management Review*, 44: 480–492.

Etzioni, A. 1961. *Comparative analysis of complex organizations*. New York: Free Press of Glencoe.

Evan, W. 1972. An organization-set model of interorganizational relations. In M. F. Tuite, R. K. Chisholm, & M. Radnor (Eds.), *Interorganizational decision making*: 181–200. Chicago: Aldine.

Evan, W. M. 1965. Toward a theory of inter-organizational relations. *Management Science*, 11(10): B217–B230.

Fama, E. F. 1980. Agency problems and the theory of the firm. *Journal of Political Economy*, 88: 288–307.

Farjoun, M., Ansell, C., & Boin, A. 2015. Pragmatism in organization studies: Meeting the challenges of a dynamic and complex world. *Organization Science*, 26: 1787–1804.

Fay, B. 2003. Phenomenology and social inquiry: From consciousness to culture and critique. In S. P. Turner & P. A. Roth (Eds.), *The Blackwell guide to the philosophy of the social sciences*: 42–63. Malden, MA: Blackwell.

Faÿ, E., & Deslandes, G. 2023. Extending and discontinuing phenomenology with Michel Henry. In F.-X. de Vaujany, J. Aroles, & M. Pérezts (Eds.), *The Oxford handbook of phenomenologies and organization studies*: 194–214. New York: Oxford University Press.

Fayol, H. 1949. *General and industrial management*. (C. Storrs, Tran.). London: Pitman & Sons.

Feldman, M. S. 2000. Organizational routines as a source of continuous change. *Organization Science*, 11: 611–629.

Feldman, M. S. 2003. A performative perspective on stability and change in organizational routines. *Industrial and Corporate Change*, 12: 727–752.

Feldman, M. S. 2015. Theory of routine dynamics and connections to strategy as practice. In D. Golsorkhi, L. Rouleau, D. Seidl, & E. Vaara (Eds.), *Cambridge handbook of strategy as practice* (2nd ed.): 317–330. Cambridge, UK: Cambridge University Press.

Feldman, M. S. 2016. Routines as process: Past, present, and future. In J. Howard-Grenville, C. Rerup, A. Langly, & H. Tsoukas (Eds.), *Organizational routines: How they are created, maintained, and changed*: 23–46. New York: Oxford University Press.

Feldman, M. S., D'Adderio, L., Dittrich, K., & Jarzabkowski, P. (Eds.). 2019. *Routine dynamics in action: Replication and transformation. Research in the sociology of organizations*, vol. 61. Bingley, UK: Emerald Publishing Limited.

Feldman, M. S., D'Adderio, L., Pentland, B. T., Dittrich, K., Rerup, C., et al. 2021. *Cambridge handbook of routine dynamics*. Cambridge, UK: Cambridge University Press.

Feldman, M. S., & Orlikowski, W. J. 2011. Theorizing practice and practicing theory. *Organization Science*, 22: 1240–1253.

Feldman, M. S., & Pentland, B. T. 2003. Reconceptualizing organizational routines as a source of flexibility and change. *Administrative Science Quarterly*, 48: 94–121.

Feldman, M., & Worline, M. 2016. The practicality of practice theory. *Academy of Management Learning & Education*, 15: 304–324.

Felin, T., Foss, N. J., & Ployhart, R. E. 2015. The microfoundations movement in strategy and organization theory. *Academy of Management Annals*, 9: 575–632.

Felin, T., & Zenger, T. R. 2009. Entrepreneurs as theorists: On the origins of collective beliefs and novel strategies. *Strategic Entrepreneurship Journal*, 3: 127–146.

Fernhaber, S. A., & Zou, H. 2022. Advancing societal grand challenge research at the interface of entrepreneurship and international business: A review and research agenda. *Journal of Business Venturing*, 37(5): 106233.

Ferraro, F., Etzion, D., & Gehman, J. 2015. Tackling grand challenges pragmatically: Robust action revisited. *Organization Studies*, 36: 363–390.

Ferraro, F., Pfeffer, J., & Sutton, R. I. 2005. Economics language and assumptions: How theories can become self-fulfilling. *Academy of Management Review*, 30: 8–24.

Fine, G. A. (Ed.). 1995. *A second Chicago school? The development of a postwar American sociology*. Chicago: University of Chicago Press.

Fligstein, N. 1996. Markets as politics: A political-cultural approach to market institutions. *American Sociological Review*, 61: 656–673.

Fligstein, N., & McAdam, D. 2012. *A theory of fields*. Oxford, UK: Oxford University Press.

Flink, T., & Kaldewey, D. 2018. The new production of legitimacy: STI policy discourses beyond the contract metaphor. *Research Policy*, 47: 14–22.

Foldvary, F. E. 1996. *Beyond neoclassical economics: Heterodox approaches to economic theory*. Cheltenham, UK: Edward Elgar Publishing.

Follett, M. P. 1918. *The new state: Group organization the solution of popular government*. New York: Longmans, Green and Co.

Foss, N. J., & Klein, P. G. 2012. *Organizing entrepreneurial judgment: A new approach to the firm*. New York: Cambridge University Press.

Fourcade, M., & Healy, K. 2007. Moral views of market society. *Annual Review of Sociology*, 33: 285–311.

Freeman, R. E. 1984. *Strategic management: A stakeholder approach*. Boston: Pitman.

Friedland, R., & Alford, R. R. 1991. Bringing society back in: Symbols, practices and institutional contradictions. In W. W. Powell & P. J. DiMaggio (Eds.), *The new institutionalism in organizational analysis*: 232–266. Chicago: University of Chicago Press.

Friedman, M. 1953. The methodology of positive economics. *Essays in positive economics*: 3–46. Chicago: University of Chicago Press.

Furnari, S. 2014. Interstitial spaces: Microinteraction settings and the genesis of new practices between institutional fields. *Academy of Management Review*, 39: 439–462.

Gaba, V., & Joseph, J. 2013. Corporate structure and performance feedback: Aspirations and adaptation in M-form firms. *Organization Science*, 24: 1102–1119.

Gabbioneta, C., Clemente, M., & Greenwood, R. (Eds.). 2023. *Organizational wrongdoing as the "foundational" grand challenge: Consequences and impact. Research in the sociology of organizations*, vol. 85. Bingley, UK: Emerald.

Gallagher, S., & Zahavi, D. 2008. *The phenomenological mind*. New York: Routledge.

Garfinkel, H. 1967. *Studies in ethnomethodology*. Englewood Cliffs, NJ: Prentice-Hall.

Gartner, W. B., Bird, B. J., & Starr, J. A. 1992. Acting as if: Differentiating entrepreneurial from organizational behavior. *Entrepreneurship Theory and Practice*, 16: 13–32.

Garud, R., & Gehman, J. 2012. Metatheoretical perspectives on sustainability journeys: Evolutionary, relational and durational. *Research Policy*, 41: 980–995.

Garud, R., & Gehman, J. 2016. Theory evaluation, entrepreneurial processes, and performativity. *Academy of Management Review*, 41: 544–549.

Garud, R., Gehman, J., & Giuliani, A. P. 2014. Contextualizing entrepreneurial innovation: A narrative perspective. *Research Policy*, 43: 1177–1188.

Garud, R., Gehman, J., & Tharchen, T. 2018. Performativity as ongoing journeys: Implications for strategy, entrepreneurship, and innovation. *Long Range Planning*, 51: 500–509.

Gasse, Y. 1992. Elaborations on the psychology of the entrepreneur. In D. L. Sexton & J. D. Kasarda (Eds.), *The state of the art of entrepreneurship*: 57–71. Boston: PWS-Kent.

Gavetti, G., Greve, H. R., Levinthal, D. A., & Ocasio, W. 2012. The behavioral theory of the firm: Assessment and prospects. *Academy of Management Annals*, 6: 1–40.

Gavetti, G., & Levinthal, D. 2000. Looking forward and looking backward: Cognitive and experiential search. *Administrative Science Quarterly*, 45: 113–137.

Gavetti, G., & Levinthal, D. A. 2004. The strategy field from the perspective of management science: Divergent strands and possible integration. *Management Science*, 50: 1309–1318.

Gegenhuber, T., Logue, D., Hinings, C. R., & Barrett, M. (Eds.). 2022. *Digital transformation and institutional theory. Research in the sociology of organizations*, vol. 83. Bingley, UK: Emerald.

Gehman, J. 2021a. Revisiting the foundations of institutional analysis: A phenomenological perspective. In C. W. J. Steele, T. R. Hanigan, V. L. Glaser, M. Toubiana, & J. Gehman (Eds.), *Macrofoundations: Exploring the institutionally situated nature of activity. Research in the sociology of organizations*, vol. 68: 235–259. Bingley, UK: Emerald.

Gehman, J. 2021b. Searching for values in practice-driven institutionalism: Practice theory, institutional logics, and values work. In M. Lounsbury, D. A. Anderson, & P. Spee (Eds.), *On practice and institution: Theorizing the interface. Research in the sociology of organizations*, vol. 70: 139–159. Bingley, UK: Emerald Publishing Limited.

Gehman, J., Etzion, D., & Ferraro, F. 2022. Robust action: Advancing a distinctive approach to tackling grand challenges, In A. A. Gümüsay, E. Marti, H. Trittin-Ulbrich, & C. Wickert (Eds.), Organizing for societal grand challenges. *Research in the sociology of organizations*, vol. 79: 258–278.

Gehman, J., Glaser, V. L., Eisenhardt, K. M., Gioia, D., Langley, A., et al. 2018. Finding theory–method fit: A comparison of three qualitative approaches to theory building. *Journal of Management Inquiry*, 27: 284–300.

Gehman, J., & Grimes, M. 2017. Hidden badge of honor: How contextual distinctiveness affects category promotion among Certified B Corporations. *Academy of Management Journal*, 60: 2294–2320.

Gehman, J., Jarzabkowski, P., Langley, A., & Tsoukas, H. (Eds.). 2024. *Organizing beyond organizations for the common good: Confronting societal challenges through process studies*, Proceedings of the 12th International Symposium on Process Organization Studies. New York: Oxford University Press.

Gehman, J., Sharma, G., & Beveridge, 'A. 2022. Theorizing institutional entrepreneuring: Arborescent and rhizomatic assembling. *Organization Studies*, 43: 289–310.

Gehman, J., & Soublière, J.-F. 2017. Cultural entrepreneurship: From making culture to cultural making. *Innovation*, 19: 61–73.

Gehman, J., Treviño, L. K., & Garud, R. 2013. Values work: A process study of the emergence and performance of organizational values practices. *Academy of Management Journal*, 56: 84–112.

George, G., Fewer, T. J., Lazzarini, S., McGahan, A. M., & Puranam, P. 2023. Partnering for grand challenges: A review of organizational design considerations in public–private collaborations. *Journal of Management*, 50: 10–40.

George, G., Howard-Grenville, J., Joshi, A., & Tihanyi, L. 2016. Understanding and tackling societal grand challenges through management research. *Academy of Management Journal*, 59: 1880–1895.

Ghoshal, S. 2005. Bad management theories are destroying good management practices. *Academy of Management Learning and Education*, 4: 75–91.

Giddens, A. 1984. *The constitution of society: Outline of the theory of structuration.* Berkeley, CA: University of California Press.

Gioia, D. A., & Chittipeddi, K. 1991. Sensemaking and sensegiving in strategic change initiation. *Strategic Management Journal*, 12: 433–448.

Glaser, V. L. 2017. Design performances: How organizations inscribe artifacts to change routines. *Academy of Management Journal*, 60: 2126–2154.

Glynn, M. A., & D'Aunno, T. 2023. An intellectual history of institutional theory: Looking back to move forward. *Academy of Management Annals*, 17: 301–330.

Goffman, E. 1967. *Interaction ritual.* Chicago: Aldine.

Golsorkhi, D., Rouleau, L., Seidl, D., & Vaara, E. 2015. *Cambridge handbook of strategy as practice* (2nd ed.). New York: Cambridge University Press.

Granovetter, M. 1985. Economic action and social structure: The problem of embeddedness. *American Journal of Sociology*, 91: 481–510.

Granovetter, M. 2017. *Society and economy: Framework and principles.* Cambridge, MA: Harvard University Press.

Granovetter, M. S. 1973. Strength of weak ties. *American Journal of Sociology*, 78: 1360–1380.

Granovetter, M., & Swedberg, R. (Eds.). 2018. *The sociology of economic life* (3rd ed.). New York: Taylor & Francis.

Granqvist, N., Grodal, S., & Woolley, J. L. 2013. Hedging your bets: Explaining executives' market labeling strategies in nanotechnology. *Organization Science*, 24: 395–413.

Green, S. E., Li, Y., & Nohria, N. 2009. Suspended in self-spun webs of significance: A rhetorical model of institutionalization and institutionally embedded agency. *Academy of Management Journal*, 52: 11–36.

"Greenspan admits 'flaw' to Congress, predicts more economic problems." 2008, October 23. *PBS NewsHour.* https://www.pbs.org/newshour/show/greenspan-admits-flaw-to-congress-predicts-more-economic-problems.

Greenwood, R., & Hinings, C. R. 1996. Understanding radical organizational change: Bringing together the old and the new institutionalism. *Academy of Management Review*, 21: 1022–1054.

Greenwood, R., Oliver, C., Lawrence, T. B., & Meyer, R. E. (Eds.). 2017. *The Sage handbook of organizational institutionalism* (2nd ed.). Thousand Oaks, CA: Sage.

Greenwood, R., Raynard, M., Kodeih, F., Micelotta, E. R., & Lounsbury, M. 2011. Institutional complexity and organizational responses. *Academy of Management Annals*, 5: 317–371.

Greve, H. R. 1998. Performance, aspirations, and risky organizational change. *Administrative Science Quarterly*, 43: 58–86.

Greve, H. R. 2003. A behavioral theory of R&D expenditures and innovations: Evidence from shipbuilding. *Academy of Management Journal*, 46: 685–702.

Greve, H. R., & Zhang, C. M. 2022. Is there a strategic organization in the behavioral theory of the firm? Looking back and looking forward. *Strategic Organization*, 20: 698–708.

Gross, N. 2003. Richard Rorty's pragmatism: A case study in the sociology of ideas. *Theory and Society*, 32: 93–148.

Gross, N. 2009. A pragmatist theory of social mechanisms. *American Sociological Review*, 74: 358–379.

Gross, N., Reed, I. A., & Winship, C. (Eds.). 2022. *The new pragmatist sociology: Inquiry, agency, and democracy*. New York: Columbia University Press.

Gulati, R., Nohria, N., & Zaheer, A. 2000. Strategic networks. *Strategic Management Journal*, 21: 203–215.

Gulati, R., & Sytch, M. 2007. Dependence asymmetry and joint dependence in interorganizational relationships: Effects of embeddedness on a manufacturer's performance in procurement relationships. *Administrative Science Quarterly*, 52: 32–69.

Gümüsay, A. A., Marti, E., Trittin-Ulbrich, H., & Wickert, C. (Eds.). 2022. *Organizing for societal grand challenges. Research in the sociology of organizations*, vol 79. Bingley, UK: Emerald.

Gümüsay, A. A., & Reinecke, J. 2022. Researching for desirable futures: From real utopias to imagining alternatives. *Journal of Management Studies*, 59: 236–242.

Gümüsay, A. A., Smets, M., & Morris, T. 2020. "God at work": Engaging central and incompatible institutional logics through elastic hybridity. *Academy of Management Journal*, 63: 124–154.

Håkansson, H., & Snehota, I. 1989. No business is an island: The network concept of business strategy. *Scandinavian Journal of Management*, 5: 187–200.

Hamann, R., Luiz, J., Ramaboa, K., Khan, F., Dhlamini, X., et al. 2020. Neither colony nor enclave: Calling for dialogical contextualism in management and organization studies. *Organization Theory*, 1(1): 2631787719879705.

Hambrick, D. C. 1994. What if the academy actually mattered? *Academy of Management Review*, 19: 11–16.

Hambrick, D. C., & Mason, P. A. 1984. Upper echelons: The organization as a reflection of its top managers. *Academy of Management Review*, 9: 193–206.

Hannan, M. T., & Freeman, J. H. 1977. The population ecology of organizations. *American Journal of Sociology*, 82: 929–964.

Hannigan, T. R. 2023. Relational publics: Studying organizational possibilities. *Organization Studies*, 44: 1899–1902.

Hannigan, T. R., Briggs, A. R., Valadao, R., Seidel, M.-D. L., & Jennings, P. D. 2022. A new tool for policymakers: Mapping cultural possibilities in an emerging ai entrepreneurial ecosystem. *Research Policy*, 51(9): 104315.

Hannigan, T. R., Pak, Y., & Jennings, P. D. 2022. Mapping the multiverse: A cultural cartographic approach to realizing entrepreneurial possibilities. In C. Lockwood & J.-F. Soublière (Eds.), *Advances in cultural entrepreneurship. Research in the sociology of organizations*, vol. 80: 217–237. Bingley, UK: Emerald Publishing Limited.

Hardy, C., & Maguire, S. 2008. Institutional entrepreneurship. In R. Greenwood, C. Oliver, R. Suddaby, & K. Sahlin (Eds.), *The Sage handbook of organizational institutionalism*: 198–217. Thousand Oaks, CA: Sage.

Hardy, C., & Maguire, S. 2017. Institutional entrepreneurship and change in fields. In R. Greenwood, C. Oliver, T. B. Lawrence, & R. E. Meyer (Eds.), *The Sage handbook of organizational institutionalism* (2nd ed.): 261–280. Thousand Oaks, CA: Sage.

Hatch, M. J. 2018. *Organization theory: Modern, symbolic, and postmodern perspectives* (4th ed.). Oxford, UK: Oxford University Press.

Haveman, H. A. 2022. *The power of organizations: A new approach to organizational theory.* Princeton, NJ: Princeton University Press.

Haveman, H. A., & Rao, H. 1997. Structuring a theory of moral sentiments; institutional and organizational coevolution in the early thrift industry. *American Journal of Sociology*, 102: 1606–1651.

Haynes, K. T., & Hillman, A. 2010. The effect of board capital and CEO power on strategic change. *Strategic Management Journal*, 31: 1145–1163.

Hedberg, L. M., & Lounsbury, M. 2021. Not just small potatoes: Cultural entrepreneurship in the moralizing of markets. *Organization Science*, 32: 433–454.

Heidegger, M. 1962. *Being and time.* (J. Macquarrie & E. Robinson, Trans.). Oxford, UK: Blackwell.

Helfat, C. E., Finkelstein, S., Mitchell, W., Peteraf, M. A., Singh, H., et al. 2007. *Dynamic capabilities: Understanding strategic change in organizations.* Malden, MA: Blackwell.

Henderson, R. 2020. *Reimagining capitalism in a world on fire.* New York: PublicAffairs.

Hernandez, M., & Haack, P. 2023. Theorizing for positive impact. *Academy of Management Review*, 48: 371–378.

Hiatt, S. R., Grandy, J. B., & Lee, B. H. 2015. Organizational responses to public and private politics: An analysis of climate change activists and U.S. oil and gas firms. *Organization Science*, 26: 1769–1786.

Hickson, D. J., Hinings, C. R., Lee, C. A., Schneck, R. E., & Pennings, J. M. 1971. A strategic contingencies' theory of intraorganizational power. *Administrative Science Quarterly*, 16: 216–229.

Hietschold, N., Voegtlin, C., Scherer, A. G., & Gehman, J. 2023. Pathways to social value and social change: An integrative review of the social entrepreneurship literature. *International Journal of Management Reviews*, 25: 564–586.

Hillman, A. J. 2005. Politicians on the board of directors: Do connections affect the bottom line? *Journal of Management*, 31: 464–481.

Hillman, A. J., & Hitt, M. A. 1999. Corporate political strategy formulation: A model of approach, participation, and strategy decisions. *Academy of Management Review*, 24: 825–842.

Hillman, A. J., Shropshire, C., & Cannella, A. A. 2007. Organizational predictors of women on corporate boards. *Academy of Management Journal*, 50: 941–952.

Hillman, A. J., Withers, M. C., & Collins, B. J. 2009. Resource dependence theory: A review. *Journal of Management*, 35: 1404–1427.

Hillman, A. J., Zardkoohi, A., & Bierman, L. 1999. Corporate political strategies and firm performance: Indications of firm-specific benefits from personal service in the U.S. government. *Strategic Management Journal*, 20: 67–81.

Hinings, B., & Meyer, R. E. 2018. *Starting points: Intellectual and institutional foundations of organization theory.* New York: Cambridge University Press.

Hinings, C. R., & Greenwood, R. 2002. Disconnects and consequences in organization theory? *Administrative Science Quarterly*, 47: 411–421.

Hirsch, P. M. 1972. Processing fads and fashions: An organization set analysis of cultural industry systems. *American Journal of Sociology*, 77: 639–659.

Hirsch, P. M., & Lounsbury, M. 1997. Ending the family quarrel: Toward a reconciliation of old and new institutionalisms. *American Behavioral Scientist*, 40: 406–418.

Hirschman, D., & Reed, I. A. 2014. Formation stories and causality in sociology: *Sociological Theory*, 32: 259–282.

Hoffman, A. J. 2021a. *The engaged scholar: Expanding the impact of academic research in today's world.* Stanford, CA: Stanford University Press.

Hoffman, A. J. 2021b. *Management as a calling: Leading business, serving society.* Stanford, CA: Stanford University Press.

Hofstede, G. 1980. *Culture's consequences: International differences in work-related values.* Beverly Hills, CA: Sage.

Hoselitz, B. F. 1963. Entrepreneurship and traditional elites. *Explorations in Entrepreneurial History*, 1(1): 36–49.

Hoskisson, R. E., Hitt, M. A., Wan, W., & Yiu, D. 1999. Theory and research in strategic management: Swings of a pendulum. *Journal of Management*, 25: 417–456.

Howard-Grenville, J., Davis, G. F., Dyllick, T., Miller, C. C., Thau, S., et al. 2019. Sustainable development for a better world: Contributions of leadership, management, and organizations. *Academy of Management Discoveries*, 5: 355–366.

Howard-Grenville, J., Nelson, A. J., Earle, A. G., Haack, J. A., & Young, D. M. 2017. "If chemists don't do it, who is going to?" Peer-driven occupational change and the emergence of green chemistry. *Administrative Science Quarterly*, 62: 524–560.

Howard-Grenville, J., & Spengler, J. 2022. Surfing the grand challenges wave in management scholarship: How did we get here, where are we now, and what's next? In A. A. Gümüsay, E. Marti, H. Trittin-Ulbrich, & C. Wickert (Eds.), *Organizing for societal grand challenges. Research in the sociology of organizations*, vol. 79: 279–295. Bingley, UK: Emerald Publishing Limited.

Hsu, G., Negro, G., & Perretti, F. 2012. Hybrids in Hollywood: A study of the production and performance of genre-spanning films. *Industrial and Corporate Change*, 21: 1427–1450.

Huff, A. S. 1999. *Writing for scholarly publication.* Thousand Oaks, CA: Sage.

Hughes, E. C. 1958. *Men and their work.* Glencoe, IL: Free Press.

Hume, D. 1751. *An enquiry concerning the principles of morals.* London: A. Millar.

Husserl, E. 1970. *The crisis of European sciences and transcendental phenomenology: An introduction to phenomenological philosophy.* (D. Carr, Tran.). Evanston, IL: Northwestern University Press.

Hwang, H., & Colyvas, J. 2021. Constructed actors and constitutive institutions for a contemporary world. *Academy of Management Review*.

Hwang, H., Colyvas, J. A., & Drori, G. S. (Eds.). 2019. *Agents, actors, actorhood: Institutional perspectives on the nature of agency, action, and authority. Research in the sociology of organizations*, vol. 58. Bingley, UK: Emerald.

Ibarra, H. 1993. Network centrality, power, and innovation involvement: Determinants of technical and administrative roles. *Academy of Management Journal*, 36: 471–501.

Ingram, P., & Baum, J. A. C. 1997. Chain affiliation and the failure of Manhattan hotels, 1898–1980. *Administrative Science Quarterly*, 42: 68–102.

Ingram, P., Yue, L. Q., & Rao, H. 2010. Trouble in store: Probes, protests, and store openings by Wal-Mart, 1998–2007. *American Journal of Sociology*, 116: 53–92.

Jacobides, M. G. 2007. The inherent limits of organizational structure and the unfulfilled role of hierarchy: Lessons from a near-war. *Organization Science*, 18: 455–477.

Jakob-Sadeh, L., & Zilber, T. B. 2019. Bringing "together": Emotions and power in organizational responses to institutional complexity. *Academy of Management Journal*, 62: 1413–1443.

Jarzabkowski, P. 2004. Strategy as practice: Recursiveness, adaptation, and practices-in-use. *Organization Studies*, 25: 529–560.

Jarzabkowski, P., Balogun, J., & Seidl, D. 2007. Strategizing: The challenges of a practice perspective. *Human Relations*, 60: 5–27.

Jarzabkowski, P., & Kaplan, S. 2015. Strategy tools-in-use: A framework for understanding "technologies of rationality" in practice. *Strategic Management Journal*, 36: 537–558.

Jarzabkowski, P., Kaplan, S., Seidl, D., & Whittington, R. 2016. On the risk of studying practices in isolation: Linking what, who, and how in strategy research. *Strategic Organization*, 14: 248–259.

Jarzabkowski, P., & Spee, A. P. 2009. Strategy-as-practice: A review and future directions for the field. *International Journal of Management Reviews*, 11: 69–95.

Jensen, M., & Meckling, W. 1976. Theory of the firm: Managerial behavior, agency costs, and ownership structure. *Journal of Financial Economics*, 3: 305–360.

Jepperson, R. L. 1991. Institutions, institutional effects, and institutionalism. In W. W. Powell & P. J. DiMaggio (Eds.), *The new institutionalism in organizational analysis*: 143–163. Chicago: University of Chicago Press.

Joas, H. 1993. *Pragmatism and social theory*. Chicago: University of Chicago Press.

Joas, H. 1996. *The creativity of action*. Chicago: University of Chicago Press.

Johnson, V. 2007. What is organizational imprinting? Cultural entrepreneurship in the founding of the Paris Opera. *American Journal of Sociology*, 113: 97–127.

Kahneman, D., & Tversky, A. 1979. Prospect theory: An analysis of decision under risk. *Econometrica*, 47: 263–291.

Kaldewey, D. 2018. The grand challenges discourse: Transforming identity work in science and science policy. *Minerva*, 56: 161–182.

Kaplan, S. 2008. Framing contests: Strategy making under uncertainty. *Organization Science*, 19: 729–752.

Kaplan, S. 2015. Mixing quantitative and qualitative research. In K. D. Elsbach & R. Kramer (Eds.), *Handbook of qualitative organizational research*: 423–433. New York: Routledge.

Kaplan, S., & Orlikowski, W. J. 2013. Temporal work in strategy making. *Organization Science*, 24: 965–995.

Katila, R., Rosenberger, J. D., & Eisenhardt, K. M. 2008. Swimming with sharks: Technology ventures, defense mechanisms and corporate relationships. *Administrative Science Quarterly*, 53: 295–332.

Kaufmann, L. J., & Danner-Schröder, A. 2022. Addressing grand challenges through different forms of organizing: A literature review. In A. A. Gümüsay, E. Marti, H. Trittin-Ulbrich, & C. Wickert (Eds.), *Organizing for societal grand challenges. Research in the sociology of organizations*, vol. 79: 163–186. Emerald Publishing Limited.

Kellogg, K. C. 2009. Operating room: Relational spaces and microinstitutional change in surgery. *American Journal of Sociology*, 115: 657–711.

Kennedy, M. T. 2008. Getting counted: Markets, media, and reality. *American Sociological Review*, 73: 270–295.

Ketokivi, M., Mantere, S., & Cornelissen, J. 2017. Reasoning by analogy and the progress of theory. *Academy of Management Review*, 42: 637–658.

Khan, F. R., Munir, K. A., & Willmott, H. 2007. A dark side of institutional entrepreneurship: Soccer balls, child labour and postcolonial impoverishment. *Organization Studies*, 28: 1055–1077.

Khanagha, S., Ansari, S., Paroutis, S., & Oviedo, L. 2022. Mutualism and the dynamics of new platform creation: A study of Cisco and fog computing. *Strategic Management Journal*, 43: 476–506.

King, A. A., & Lenox, M. J. 2000. Industry self-regulation without sanctions: The chemical industry's responsible care program. *Academy of Management Journal*, 43: 698–716.

Kirzner, I. M. 1973. *Competition and entrepreneurship*. Chicago: University of Chicago Press.

Kiser, E., & Hechter, M. 1998. The debate on historical sociology: Rational choice theory and its critics. *American Journal of Sociology*, 104: 785–816.

Kistruck, G. M., & Slade Shantz, A. 2022. Research on grand challenges: Adopting an abductive experimentation methodology. *Organization Studies*, 43: 1479–1505.

Kogut, B., & Zander, U. 1992. Knowledge of the firm, combinative capabilities, and the replication of technology. *Organization Science*, 3: 383–397.

Kotiloglu, S., Chen, Y., & Lechler, T. 2021. Organizational responses to performance feedback: A meta-analytic review. *Strategic Organization*, 19: 285–311.

Kraatz, M. S., & Block, E. 2008. Organizational implications of institutional pluralism. In R. Greenwood, C. Oliver, R. Suddaby, & K. Sahlin-Andersson (Eds.), *The Sage handbook of organizational institutionalism*: 243–275. Thousand Oaks, CA: Sage.

Kuhn, T. S. 1970. *The structure of scientific revolutions* (2nd ed.). Chicago: University of Chicago Press.

Kuusela, P., Keil, T., & Maula, M. 2017. Driven by aspirations, but in what direction? Performance shortfalls, slack resources, and resource-consuming vs. resource-freeing organizational change. *Strategic Management Journal*, 38: 1101–1120.

Kwon, S.-W., Rondi, E., Levin, D. Z., De Massis, A., & Brass, D. J. 2020. Network brokerage: An integrative review and future research agenda. *Journal of Management*, 46: 1092–1120.

Lakatos, I. 1970. Falsification and the methodology of scientific research programmes. In I. Lakatos & A. Musgrave (Eds.), *Criticism and the growth of knowledge: Proceedings of the International Colloquium in the Philosophy of Science, London, 1965*, vol. 4: 91–196. Cambridge, UK: Cambridge University Press.

Langley, A. 1999. Strategies for theorizing from process data. *Academy of Management Review*, 24: 691–710.

Langley, A., Smallman, C., Tsoukas, H., & Van de Ven, A. H. 2013. Process studies of change in organization and management: Unveiling temporality, activity, and flow. *Academy of Management Journal*, 56: 1–13.

Langley, A., & Tsoukas, H. 2016. *The Sage handbook of process organization studies*. Thousand Oaks, CA: Sage.

Langlois, R. N. 1992. Transaction-cost economics in real time. *Industrial and Corporate Change*, 1: 99–127.

Lant, T. K., & Mezias, S. J. 1992. An organizational learning model of convergence and reorientation. *Organization Science*, 3: 47–71.

Latour, B. 1986. The powers of association. In J. Law (Ed.), *Power, action and belief*: 264–280. London: Routledge.

Latour, B. 1987. *Science in action*. Cambridge, MA: Harvard University Press.

Latour, B. 2005. *Reassembling the social*. New York: Oxford University Press.

Law, J., & Hassard, J. (Eds.). 1999. *Actor network theory and after*. Malden, MA: Blackwell.

Lawlor, L. 2003. *Thinking through French philosophy*. Bloomington, IN: Indiana University Press.

Lawrence, P. R., & Lorsch, J. W. 1967. Differentiation and integration in complex organizations. *Administrative Science Quarterly*, 12: 1–47.

Lawrence, T. B. 2008. Power, institutions and organizations. In R. Greenwood, C. Oliver, R. Suddaby, & K. Sahlin (Eds.), *The Sage handbook of organizational institutionalism*: 170–197. Thousand Oaks, CA: Sage.

Lawrence, T. B., Leca, B., & Zilber, T. B. 2013. Institutional work: Current research, new directions and overlooked issues. *Organization Studies*, 34: 1023–1033.

Lawrence, T. B., & Phillips, N. 2019. *Constructing organizational life: How social-symbolic work shapes selves, organizations, and institutions*. Oxford, UK: Oxford University Press.

Lawrence, T. B., & Suddaby, R. 2006. Institutions and institutional work. In S. R. Clegg, C. Hardy, T. B. Lawrence, & W. R. Nord (Eds.), *The Sage handbook of organization studies*, vol. 2: 215–254. Thousand Oaks, CA: Sage.

Lê, J., & Spee, P. 2015. The role of materiality in the practice of strategy. In D. Golsorkhi, L. Rouleau, D. Seidl, & E. Vaara (Eds.), *Cambridge handbook of strategy as practice* (2nd ed.): 582–597. New York: Cambridge University Press.

Leahey, E., Beckman, C. M., & Stanko, T. L. 2017. Prominent but less productive: The impact of interdisciplinarity on scientists' research. *Administrative Science Quarterly*, 62: 105–139.

Learmonth, M. 2008. Speaking out: Evidence-based management: A backlash against pluralism in organizational studies? *Organization*, 15: 283–291.

Learned, E. P., Christensen, C. R., Andrews, K. R., & Guth, W. D. 1969. *Business policy: Text and cases*. Homewood, IL: Irwin.

Lee, B. H., Hiatt, S. R., & Lounsbury, M. 2017. Market mediators and the trade-offs of legitimacy-seeking behaviors in a nascent category. *Organization Science*, 28: 447–470.

Lee, M.-D. P., & Lounsbury, M. 2015. Filtering institutional logics: Community logic variation and differential responses to the institutional complexity of toxic waste. *Organization Science*, 26: 847–866.

Legg, C., & Hookway, C. 2021. Pragmatism. In E. N. Zalta (Ed.), *The Stanford encyclopedia of philosophy* (Summer 2021). Stanford University. https://plato.stanford.edu/archives/sum2021/entries/pragmatism/.

Leibenstein, H. 1966. Allocative efficiency vs. "X-efficiency." *American Economic Review*, 56: 392–415.

Leifer, E. M. 1991. *Actors as observers: A theory of skill in social relationships*. New York: Garland.

Leonardi, P. M. 2011. When flexible routines meet flexible technologies: Affordance, constraint, and the imbrication of human and material agencies. *MIS Quarterly*, 35: 147–167.

Leonardi, P. M., & Barley, S. R. 2010. What's under construction here? Social action, materiality, and power in constructivist studies of technology and organizing. *Academy of Management Annals*, 4: 1–51.

Leonardi, P. M., Nardi, B. A., & Kallinikos, J. 2012. *Materiality and organizing: Social interaction in a technological world*. New York: Oxford University Press.

Lévi-Strauss, C. 1966. *The savage mind*. Chicago: University of Chicago Press.

Levitt, B., & March, J. G. 1988. Organizational learning. *Annual Review of Sociology*, 14: 319–340.

Locke, K., & Golden-Biddle, K. 1997. Constructing opportunities for contribution: Structuring intertextual coherence and problematizing in organizational studies. *Academy of Management Journal*, 40: 1023–1062.

Locke, R. M. 2013. *The promise and limits of private power: Promoting labor standards in a global economy*. New York: Cambridge University Press.

Lockwood, C., & Soublière, J.-F. (Eds.). 2022. *Advances in cultural entrepreneurship. Research in the sociology of organizations,* vol. 80. Bingley, UK: Emerald.

Lok, J., & Willmott, H. 2019. Embedded agency in institutional theory: Problem or paradox? *Academy of Management Review*, 44: 470–473.

Lorino, P. 2018. *Pragmatism and Organization Studies*. Oxford, UK: Oxford University Press.

Lounsbury, M. 1998. Collective entrepreneurship: The mobilization of college and university recycling coordinators. *Journal of Organizational Change Management*, 11: 50–69.

Lounsbury, M. 2001. Institutional sources of practice variation: Staffing college and university recycling programs. *Administrative Science Quarterly*, 46: 29–56.

Lounsbury, M. 2002. Institutional transformation and status mobility: The professionalization of the field of finance. *Academy of Management Journal*, 45: 255–266.

Lounsbury, M. 2007. A tale of two cities: Competing logics and practice variation in the professionalization of mutual funds. *Academy of Management Journal*, 50: 289–307.

Lounsbury, M. 2008. Institutional rationality and practice variation: New directions in the institutional analysis of practice. *Accounting, Organizations and Society*, 33: 349–361.

Lounsbury, M., Anderson, D. A., & Spee, P. (Eds.). 2021. *On practice and institution: Theorizing the interface. Research in the sociology of organizations*, vol. 71. Bingley, UK: Emerald Publishing Limited.

Lounsbury, M., & Crumley, E. T. 2007. New practice creation: An institutional perspective on innovation. *Organization Studies*, 28: 993–1012.

Lounsbury, M., Gehman, J., & Glynn, M. A. 2019. Beyond homo entrepreneurus: Judgment and the theory of cultural entrepreneurship. *Journal of Management Studies*, 56: 1214–1236.

Lounsbury, M., & Glynn, M. A. 2001. Cultural entrepreneurship: Stories, legitimacy, and the acquisition of resources. *Strategic Management Journal*, 22: 545–564.

Lounsbury, M., & Glynn, M. A. 2019. *Cultural entrepreneurship: A new agenda for the study of entrepreneurial processes and possibilities*. New York: Cambridge University Press.

Lounsbury, M., Steele, C. W. J., Wang, M. S., & Toubiana, M. 2021. New directions in the study of institutional logics: From tools to phenomena. *Annual Review of Sociology*, 47: 261–280.

Lounsbury, M., & Ventresca, M. 2003. The new structuralism in organizational theory. *Organization*, 10: 457–480.

Lounsbury, M., Ventresca, M., & Hirsch, P. M. 2003. Social movements, field frames and industry emergence: A cultural-political perspective on us recycling. *Socio-Economic Review*, 1: 71–104.

Lounsbury, M., & Wang, M. S. 2020. Into the clearing: Back to the future of constitutive institutional analysis. *Organization Theory*, 1(1): 2631787719891173.

Lucas, D. S., Grimes, M. G., & Gehman, J. 2022. Remaking capitalism: The strength of weak legislation in mobilizing B Corporation certification. *Academy of Management Journal*, 65: 958–987.

Luckmann, T. 1983. *Life-world and social realities*. Portsmouth, NH: Heinemann.

MacIntyre, A. 1981. *After virtue: A study in moral theory*. Notre Dame, IN: University of Notre Dame Press.

MacKenzie, D., & Millo, Y. 2003. Constructing a market, performing theory: The historical sociology of a financial derivatives exchange. *American Journal of Sociology*, 109: 107–145.

Mair, J., & Hehenberger, L. 2014. Front-stage and backstage convening: The transition from opposition to mutualistic coexistence in organizational philanthropy. *Academy of Management Journal*, 57: 1174–1200.

Mair, J., Martí, I., & Ventresca, M. J. 2012. Building inclusive markets in rural Bangladesh: How intermediaries work institutional voids. *Academy of Management Journal*, 55: 819–850.

Maitlis, S. 2005. The social processes of organizational sensemaking. *Academy of Management Journal*, 48: 21–49.

Maitlis, S., & Christianson, M. 2014. Sensemaking in organizations: Taking stock and moving forward. *Academy of Management Annals*, 8: 57–125.

Maitlis, S., & Lawrence, T. B. 2007. Triggers and enablers of sensegiving in organizations. *Academy of Management Journal*, 50: 57–84.

Mantere, S., Schildt, H. A., & Sillince, J. A. A. 2012. Reversal of strategic change. *Academy of Management Journal*, 55: 172–196.

March, J. G. 1989. *Decisions and organizations*. New York: Blackwell.

March, J. G. 2006. Rationality, foolishness, and adaptive intelligence. *Strategic Management Journal*, 27: 201–214.

March, J. G. 1991. Exploration and exploitation in organizational learning. *Organization Science*, 2: 71–87.

March, J. G., & Simon, H. A. 1958. *Organizations*. New York: Wiley & Sons.

Margolis, J. D., & Walsh, J. P. 2003. Misery loves companies: Rethinking social initiatives by business. *Administrative Science Quarterly*, 48: 268–305.

Marquis, C. 2020. *Better business: How the B Corp movement is remaking capitalism*. New Haven, CT: Yale University Press.

Marshall, A. 1890. *Principles of economics*. London: Macmillan.

Martens, M. L., Jennings, J. E., & Jennings, P. D. 2007. Do the stories they tell get them the money they need? The role of entrepreneurial narratives in resource acquisition. *Academy of Management Journal*, 50: 1107–1132.

Marti, E., & Gond, J.-P. 2018. When do theories become self-fulfilling? Exploring the boundary conditions of performativity. *Academy of Management Review*, 43: 487–508.

Martín, E. 2014. How to write a good article. *Current Sociology*, 62: 949–955.

Mason, E. S. 1939. Price and production policies of large-scale enterprise. *American Economic Review*, 29: 61–74.

Mason, E. S. 1957. *Economic concentration and the monopoly problem*. Cambridge, MA: Harvard University Press.

Mayhew, B. H. 1980. Structuralism versus individualism: Part 1, shadowboxing in the dark. *Social Forces*, 59: 335–375.

McAdam, D., McCarthy, J. D., & Zald, M. N. 1996. *Comparative perspectives on social movements: Political opportunities, mobilizing structures, and cultural framings*. Cambridge, UK: Cambridge University Press.

McCarthy, J. D., & Zald, M. N. 1977. Resource mobilization and social movements: A partial theory. *American Journal of Sociology*, 82: 1212–1241.

McDonnell, M.-H., & King, B. 2013. Keeping up appearances: Reputational threat and impression management after social movement boycotts. *Administrative Science Quarterly*, 58: 387–419.

McDonnell, M.-H., King, B. G., & Soule, S. A. 2015. A dynamic process model of private politics: Activist targeting and corporate receptivity to social challenges. *American Sociological Review*, 80: 654–678.

McGahan, A. M. 2018. 2017 Presidential address. Freedom in scholarship: Lessons from Atlanta. *Academy of Management Review*, 43: 173–178.

McGrath, J. E. 1982. Dilemmatics: The study of research choices and dilemmas. In J. E. McGrath, J. Martin, & R. A. Kulka (Eds.), *Judgment calls in research*: 69–101. Beverly Hills, CA: Sage.

McInerney, P.-B. 2014. *From social movement to moral market: How the circuit riders sparked an IT revolution and created a technology market*. Stanford, CA: Stanford University Press.

McKay, R. B. 2001. Organizational responses to an environmental bill of rights. *Organization Studies*, 22: 625–658.

McPherson, C. M., & Sauder, M. 2013. Logics in action: Managing institutional complexity in a drug court. *Administrative Science Quarterly*, 58: 165–196.

Mead, G. H. 1934. *Mind, self, and society*. Chicago: University of Chicago Press.

Merleau-Ponty, M. 1964. *The primacy of perception*. (J. M. Edie, Ed.). Evanston, IL: Northwestern University Press.

Merleau-Ponty, M. 2012. *Phenomenology of perception*. (D. A. Landes, Tran.). New York: Routledge.

Meyer, J. W. 2008. Reflections on institutional theories of organizations. In R. Greenwood, C. Oliver, R. Suddaby, & K. Sahlin (Eds.), *The Sage handbook of organizational institutionalism*: 788–809. Thousand Oaks, CA: Sage.

Meyer, J. W. 2010. World society, institutional theories, and the actor. *Annual Review of Sociology*, 36: 1–20.

Meyer, J. W., Boli, J., & Thomas, G. M. 1987. Ontology and rationalization in the Western cultural account. In G. M. Thomas, J. W. Meyer, F. O. Ramirez, & J. Boli (Eds.), *Institutional structure: Constituting state, society and the individual*: 12–37. Thousand Oaks, CA: Sage.

Meyer, J. W., Boli, J., Thomas, G. M., & Ramirez, F. O. 1997. World society and the nation-state. *American Journal of Sociology*, 103: 144–181.

Meyer, J. W., & Jepperson, R. L. 2000. The 'actors' of modern society: The cultural construction of social agency. *Sociological Theory*, 18: 100–120.

Meyer, J. W., & Rowan, B. 1977. Institutionalized organizations: Formal structure as myth and ceremony. *American Journal of Sociology*, 83: 340–363.

Meyer, J. W., & Scott, W. R. 1983. *Organizational environments: Ritual and rationality*. Beverly Hills, CA: Sage.

Meyer, R. E. 2008. New sociology of knowledge: Historical legacy and contributions to current debates in institutional research. In R. Greenwood, C. Oliver, R. Suddaby, & K. Sahlin (Eds.), *The Sage handbook of organizational institutionalism*: 519–538. Thousand Oaks, CA: Sage.

Meyer, R. E., & Vaara, E. 2020. Institutions and actorhood as co-constitutive and co-constructed: The argument and areas for future research. *Journal of Management Studies*, 57: 898–910.

Meyerson, D. E., & Scully, M. A. 1995. Tempered radicalism and the politics of ambivalence and change. *Organization Science*, 6: 585–600.

Micelotta, E., Lounsbury, M., & Greenwood, R. 2017. Pathways of institutional change: An integrative review and research agenda. *Journal of Management*, 43: 1885–1910.

Mill, J. S. 1863. *Utilitarianism*. London: Parker, Son, and Bourn.

Milliken, F. J. 1987. Three types of perceived uncertainty about the environment: State, effect, and response uncertainty. *Academy of Management Review*, 12: 133–143.

Miner, A. S., & Mezias, S. J. 1996. Ugly duckling no more: Pasts and futures of organizational learning research. *Organization Science*, 7: 88–99.

Mintzberg, H. 1978. Patterns in strategy formation. *Management Science*, 24: 934–948.

Mizruchi, M. S. 1982. *The American corporate network 1904–1974*. Beverly Hills, CA: Sage.

Moran, D. 2005. *Edmund Husserl: Founder of phenomenology*. Malden, MA: Polity.

Moreno, J. L. 1953. *Who shall survive? Foundations of sociometry, group psycho-therapy and sociodrama*. Beacon, NY: Beacon House.

Morgan, G. 1980. Paradigms, metaphors, and puzzle solving in organization theory. *Administrative Science Quarterly*, 25: 605–622.

Moustakas, C. 1994. *Phenomenological research methods*. Thousand Oaks, CA: Sage.

Munir, K. A. 2015. A loss of power in institutional theory. *Journal of Management Inquiry*, 24: 90–92.

Muradian, R., & Gómez-Baggethun, E. 2021. Beyond ecosystem services and nature's contributions: Is it time to leave utilitarian environmentalism behind? *Ecological Economics*, 185: 107038.

Navis, C., & Glynn, M. A. 2010. How new market categories emerge: Temporal dynamics of legitimacy, identity, and entrepreneurship in satellite radio, 1990–2005. *Administrative Science Quarterly*, 55: 439–471.

Navis, C., & Glynn, M. A. 2011. Legitimate distinctiveness and the entrepreneurial identity: Influence on investor judgments of new venture plausibility. *Academy of Management Review*, 36: 479–499.

Nelsen, B. J., & Barley, S. R. 1997. For love or money? Commodification and the construction of an occupational mandate. *Administrative Science Quarterly*, 42: 619–653.

Nelson, R. R., & Winter, S. G. 1982. *An evolutionary theory of economic change*. Cambridge, MA: Harvard University Press.

Nelson, R. R., & Winter, S. G. 2002. Evolutionary theorizing in economics. *Journal of Economic Perspectives*, 16(2): 23–46.

Nicolini, D. 2011. Practice as the site of knowing: Insights from the field of tele-medicine. *Organization Science*, 22: 602–620.

Nicolini, D., Gherardi, S., & Yanow, D. 2003. *Knowing in organizations: A practice-based approach*. Armonk, NY: M. E. Sharpe.

Nicolini, D., & Monteiro, P. 2016. The practice approach: For a praxeology of organisational and management studies. In A. Langley & H. Tsoukas (Eds.), *The Sage handbook of process organization studies*: 110–126. Thousand Oaks, CA: Sage.

Nigam, A., & Ocasio, W. 2010. Event attention, environmental sensemaking, and change in institutional logics: An inductive analysis of the effects of public attention to Clinton's health care reform initiative. *Organization Science*, 21: 823–841.

Nilakant, V., & Rao, H. 1994. Agency theory and uncertainty in organizations: An evaluation. *Organization Studies*, 15: 649–672.

Obstfeld, D. 2005. Social networks, the tertius iungens and orientation involve-ment in innovation. *Administrative Science Quarterly*, 50: 100–130.

Ocasio, W. 1994. Political dynamics and the circulation of power: CEO succession in U.S. industrial corporations, 1960–1990. *Administrative Science Quarterly*, 39: 285–312.

Ocasio, W. 1997. Towards an attention-based view of the firm. *Strategic Management Journal*, 18: 187–206.

Ocasio, W. 1999. Institutionalized action and corporate governance: The reliance on rules of CEO succession. *Administrative Science Quarterly*, 44: 384–416.

Ocasio, W. 2023. Institutions and their social construction: A cross-level perspective. *Organization Theory*, 4(3): 26317877231194368.

Ocasio, W., Thornton, P. H., & Lounsbury, M. 2017. Advances to the institutional logics perspective. In R. Greenwood, C. Oliver, T. B. Lawrence, & R. E. Meyer (Eds.), *The Sage handbook of organizational institutionalism* (2nd ed.): 509–531. Thousand Oaks, CA: Sage.

Odziemkowska, K. 2022. Frenemies: Overcoming audiences' ideological opposition to firm–activist collaborations. *Administrative Science Quarterly*, 67: 469–514.

O'Leary, M., & Chia, R. 2007. Epistemes and structures of sensemaking in organizational life. *Journal of Management Inquiry*, 16: 392–406.

Oliver, C. 1991. Strategic responses to institutional processes. *Academy of Management Review*, 16: 145–179.

Olson, M. 1996. Distinguished lecture on economics in government: Big bills left on the sidewalk: Why some nations are rich, and others poor. *Journal of Economic Perspectives*, 10(2): 3–24.

Orlikowski, W. J. 2000. Using technology and constituting structures: A practice lens for studying technology in organizations. *Organization Science*, 11: 404–428.

Orlikowski, W. J. 2007. Sociomaterial practices: Exploring technology at work. *Organization Studies*, 28: 1435–1448.

Orlikowski, W. J., & Scott, S. V. 2008. Sociomateriality: Challenging the separation of technology, work and organization. *Academy of Management Annals*, 2: 433–474.

Orlikowski, W. J., Yates, J., Okamura, K., & Fujimoto, M. 1995. Shaping electronic communication: The metastructuring of technology in the context of use. *Organization Science*, 6: 423–444.

Pache, A.-C., & Santos, F. 2013. Inside the hybrid organization: Selective coupling as a response to competing institutional logics. *Academy of Management Journal*, 56: 972–1001.

Padgett, J. F., & Ansell, C. K. 1993. Robust action and the rise of the Medici, 1400–1434. *American Journal of Sociology*, 98: 1259–1319.

Padgett, J. F., & Powell, W. W. 2012. The problem of emergence. In J. F. Padgett & W. W. Powell (Eds.), *The emergence of organizations and markets*: 1–29. Princeton, NJ: Princeton University Press.

Parmar, B. L., Phillips, R., & Freeman, R. E. 2016. Pragmatism and organization studies. In R. Mir, H. Willmott, & M. Greenwood (Eds.), *The Routledge companion to philosophy in organization studies*: 199–211. New York: Routledge.

Patriotta, G. 2003. Sensemaking on the shop floor: Narratives of knowledge in organizations. *Journal of Management Studies*, 40: 349–375.

Pennings, J. M. 1982. Organizational birth frequencies: An empirical investigation. *Administrative Science Quarterly*, 27: 120–144.

Peredo, A. M., & McLean, M. 2013. Indigenous development and the cultural captivity of entrepreneurship. *Business & Society*, 52: 592–620.

Perrow, C. 1986. *Complex organizations: A critical essay*. New York: Random House.

Perrow, C. 1991. A society of organizations. *Theory and Society*, 20: 725–762.

Pettigrew, A. M. 1973. *The politics of organizational decision-making*. London: Tavistock.

Pettigrew, A. M. 1992. The character and significance of strategy process research. *Strategic Management Journal*, 13: 5–16.

Pettit, P. 2005. Rawls's political ontology. *Politics, Philosophy & Economics*, 4: 157–174.

Pfeffer, J. 1993. Barriers to the advance of organizational science: Paradigm development as a dependent variable. *Academy of Management Review*, 18: 599–620.

Pfeffer, J., & Salancik, G. R. 1978. *The external control of organizations*. New York: Harper & Row.

Pillai, S. D., Goldfarb, B., & Kirsch, D. A. 2020. The origins of firm strategy: Learning by economic experimentation and strategic pivots in the early automobile industry. *Strategic Management Journal*, 41: 369–399.

Polanyi, K. 1944. *The great transformation*. New York: Farrar & Rinehart.

Pollock, T. G., Lashley, K., Rindova, V. P., & Han, J.-H. 2019. Which of these things are not like the others? Comparing the rational, emotional, and moral aspects of reputation, status, celebrity, and stigma. *Academy of Management Annals*, 13: 444–478.

Porter, A. J., Tuertscher, P., & Huysman, M. 2020. Saving our oceans: Scaling the impact of robust action through crowdsourcing. *Journal of Management Studies*, 57: 246–286.

Porter, M. E. 1980. *Competitive strategy: Techniques of industry and competitor analysis*. New York: Free Press.

Porter, M. E. 1981. The contributions of industrial organization to strategic management. *Academy of Management Review*, 6: 609–620.

Porter, M. E. 1985. *Competitive advantage: Creating and sustaining superior performance*. New York: Free Press.

Portes, A., & Jensen, L. 1989. The enclave and the entrants: Patterns of ethnic enterprise in Miami before and after Mariel. *American Sociological Review*, 54: 929–949.

Portes, A., & Zhou, M. 1996. Self-employment and the earnings of immigrants. *American Sociological Review*, 61: 219–230.

Powell, W. W. 1990. Neither market nor hierarchy: Network forms of organization. *Research in Organizational Behavior*, 12: 295–336.

Powell, W. W., & DiMaggio, P. J. 1991. *The new institutionalism in organizational analysis*. Chicago: University of Chicago Press.

Powell, W. W., Koput, K. W., & Smith-Doerr, L. 1996. Interorganizational collaboration and the locus of innovation: Networks of learning in biotechnology. *Administrative Science Quarterly*, 41: 116–145.

Powell, W. W., White, D. R., Koput, K. W., & Owen-Smith, J. 2005. Network dynamics and field evolution: The growth of interorganizational collaboration in the life sciences. *American Journal of Sociology*, 110: 1132–1205.

Pratt, M. G. 2000. The good, the bad, and the ambivalent: Managing identification among Amway distributors. *Administrative Science Quarterly*, 45: 456–493.

Prior, A. 2014, November 2. What college can teach the aspiring entrepreneur. *Wall Street Journal*.

Pugh, D. S., & Hickson, D. J. 2007. Derek Pugh and the Aston Group, including John Child and David Hickson. In *Writers on organizations* (6th ed): 8–12. Thousand Oaks, CA: Sage.

Pugh, D. S., Hickson, D. J., & Hinings, C. R. 1969. An empirical taxonomy of structures of work organizations. *Administrative Science Quarterly*, 14: 115–126.

Pugh, D. S., Hickson, D. J., Hinings, C. R., & Turner, C. 1968. Dimensions of organization structure. *Administrative Science Quarterly*, 13: 65–105.

Quattrone, P. 2015. Governing social orders, unfolding rationality, and Jesuit accounting practices: A procedural approach to institutional logics. *Administrative Science Quarterly*, 60: 411–445.

Rao, H. 1998. Caveat emptor: The construction of nonprofit consumer watchdog organizations. *American Journal of Sociology*, 103: 912–961.

Rao, H., Monin, P., & Durand, R. 2003. Institutional change in Toque Ville: Nouvelle cuisine as an identity movement in French gastronomy. *American Journal of Sociology*, 108: 795–843.

Rao, H., Morrill, C., & Zald, M. N. 2000. Power plays: How social movements and collective action create new organizational forms. *Research in Organizational Behaviour*, 22(9), 239–282.

Rao, H., Yue, L. Q., & Ingram, P. 2011. Laws of attraction: Regulatory arbitrage in the face of activism in right-to-work states. *American Sociological Review*, 76: 365–385.

Rawls, J. 1993. *Political liberalism*. New York: Columbia University Press.

Reay, T., Berta, W., & Kohn, M. K. 2009. What's the evidence on evidence-based management? *Academy of Management Perspectives*, 23: 5–18.

Reckwitz, A. 2002. Toward a theory of social practices. *European Journal of Social Theory*, 5: 243–263.

Ref, O., & Shapira, Z. 2017. Entering new markets: The effect of performance feedback near aspiration and well below and above it. *Strategic Management Journal*, 38: 1416–1434.

Reinecke, J., Boxenbaum, E., & Gehman, J. 2022. Impactful theory: Pathways to mattering. *Organization Theory*, 3(4): 26317877221131061.

Rcrup, C. 2009. Attentional triangulation: Learning from unexpected rare crises. *Organization Science*, 20: 876–893.

Reus-Smit, C. 2018. *On cultural diversity: International theory in a world of difference*. New York: Cambridge University Press.

Rider, C. I., Wade, J. B., Swaminathan, A., & Schwab, A. 2023. Racial disparity in leadership: Evidence of valuative bias in the promotions of National Football League coaches. *American Journal of Sociology*, 129: 227–275.

Riemer, K., & Johnston, R. B. 2017. Clarifying ontological inseparability with Heidegger's analysis of equipment. *MIS Quarterly*, 41: 1059–1082.

Rindova, V., Barry, D., & Ketchen, D. J. 2009. Entrepreneuring as emancipation. *Academy of Management Review*, 34: 477–491.

Rindova, V., Dalpiaz, E., & Ravasi, D. 2011. A cultural quest: A study of organizational use of new cultural resources in strategy formation. *Organization Science*, 22: 413–431.

Rindova, V. P., & Martins, L. L. 2021. Shaping possibilities: A design science approach to developing novel strategies. *Academy of Management Review*, 46: 800–822.

Ritzer, G. (Ed.). 1992. *Metatheorizing*. Newbury Park, CA: Sage.

Rorty, R. 1979. *Philosophy and the mirror of nature* (1st ed.). Princeton, NJ: Princeton University Press.

Rorty, R. 1982. *Consequences of pragmatism (Essays: 1972–1980)*. Minneapolis, MN: University of Minnesota Press.

Rorty, R. 1989. *Contingency, irony, and solidarity*. New York: Cambridge University Press.

Rouleau, L., & Balogun, J. 2011. Middle managers, strategic sensemaking, and discursive competence. *Journal of Management Studies*, 48: 953–983.

Rousseau, D. M. (Ed.). 2012. *The Oxford handbook of evidence-based management*. New York: Oxford University Press.

Rowley, T. J. 1997. Moving beyond dyadic ties: A network theory of stakeholder influences. *Academy of Management Review*, 22: 887–910.

Ruef, M. 1999. Social ontology and the dynamics of organizational forms: Creating market actors in the healthcare field, 1966–1994. *Social Forces*, 77: 1403–1432.

Ruef, M. 2000. The emergence of organizational forms: A community ecology approach. *American Journal of Sociology*, 106: 658–714.

Ruef, M. 2010. *The entrepreneurial group: Social identities, relations, and collective action*. Princeton, NJ: Princeton University Press.

Ruef, M., Aldrich, H. E., & Carter, N. M. 2003. The structure of founding teams: Homophily, strong ties, and isolation among U.S. entrepreneurs. *American Sociological Review*, 68: 195–222.

Ruef, M., & Lounsbury, M. (Eds.). 2007. *The sociology of entrepreneurship. Research in the sociology of organizations*, vol. 25. Bingley, UK: Emerald.

Ruef, M., & Patterson, K. 2009. Credit and classification: The impact of industry boundaries in nineteenth-century America. *Administrative Science Quarterly*, 54: 486–520.

Rumelt, R., Schendel, D., & Teece, D. 1994. *Fundamental issues in strategy: A research agenda*. Boston: Harvard Business School Press.

Sahlin, K., & Eriksson-Zetterquist, U. (Eds.). 2024. *Revitalizing collegiality. Research in the sociology of organizations*, vol. 87. Bingley, UK: Emerald.

Sahlin-Andersson, K. 1996. Imitating by editing success: The construction of organizational fields. In B. Czarniawska & G. Sevón (Eds.), *Translating organizational change*: 69–92. New York: de Gruyter.

Salmon, E., Chavez, J. F., & Murphy, M. 2022. New perspectives and critical insights from Indigenous peoples' research: A systematic review of Indigenous management and organization literature. *Academy of Management Annals* 17: 439–491.

Sanchez, R., & Heene, A. 1997. Reinventing strategic management: New theory and practice for competence-based competition. *European Management Journal*, 15: 303–317.

Sandberg, J., & Tsoukas, H. 2011. Grasping the logic of practice: Theorizing through practical rationality. *Academy of Management Review*, 36: 338–360.

Sandberg, J., & Tsoukas, H. 2016. Practice theory: What it is, its philosophical base, and what it offers organization studies. In R. Mir, H. Willmott, & M. Greenwood (Eds.), *The Routledge companion to philosophy in organization studies*: 184–198. New York: Routledge.

Sarewitz, D. 2004. How science makes environmental controversies worse. *Environmental Science & Policy*, 7: 385–403.

Schatzki, T. R. 2002. *The site of the social*. University Park, PA: Pennsylvania State University Press.

Schatzki, T. R., Knorr-Cetina, K., & von Savigny, E. 2001. *The practice turn in contemporary theory*. New York: Routledge.

Schein, E. H. 1985. *Organizational culture and leadership*. San Francisco: Jossey-Bass.

Schendel, D., & Hofer, C. W. 1979. Introduction. In D. Schendel & C. W. Hofer (Eds.), *Strategic management: A new view of business policy and planning*: 1–22. Boston: Little Brown.

Scherer, A. G., & Palazzo, G. 2007. Toward a political conception of corporate responsibility: Business and society seen from a Habermasian perspective. *Academy of Management Review*, 32: 1096–1120.

Scherer, F. M., & Ross, D. 1990. *Industrial market structure and economic performance* (3rd ed.). Boston: Houghton Mifflin.

Schildt, H., Mantere, S., & Cornelissen, J. 2020. Power in sensemaking processes. *Organization Studies*, 41: 241–265.

Schiller-Merkens, S., & Balsiger, P. 2019. *The contested moralities of markets*. Bingley, UK: Emerald.

Schneiberg, M., & Clemens, E. S. 2006. The typical tools for the job: Research strategies in institutional analysis. *Sociological Theory*, 24: 195–227.

Schneiberg, M., & Lounsbury, M. 2017. Social movements and the dynamics of institutions and organizations. In R. Greenwood, C. Oliver, T. B. Lawrence, & R. E. Meyer (Eds.), *The Sage handbook of organizational institutionalism* (2nd ed.): 281–310. Thousand Oaks, CA: Sage.

Schneiberg, M., & Soule, S. A. 2005. Institutionalization as a contested, multilevel process. In G. F. Davis, D. McAdam, W. R. Scott, & M. N. Zald (Eds.), *Social movements and organization theory*: 122–160. New York: Cambridge University Press.

Schneider, A. 2023. Untaming grand challenges research: Against a de-politicization of grand challenges. *Business & Society*, 00076503231204292.

Schofer, E., Hironaka, A., Frank, D. J., & Longhofer, W. 2012. Sociological institutionalism and world society. *The Wiley-Blackwell companion to political sociology*: 57–68. Malden, MA: Wiley.

Schumpeter, J. A. 1934. *The theory of economic development*. (R. Opie, Tran.). Cambridge, MA: Harvard University Press.

Schüssler, E., Ruling, C.-C., & Wittneben, B. B. F. 2014. On melting summits: The limitations of field-configuring events as catalysts of change in transnational climate policy. *Academy of Management Journal*, 57: 140–171.

Schutz, A. 1967. *The phenomenology of the social world*. Evanston, IL: Northwestern University Press.

Schutz, A., & Luckmann, T. 1973. *The structures of the life-world* (R. M. Zaner & H. T. Engelhardt, Jr., Trans.), vol. 1. Evanston, IL: Northwestern University Press.

Schutz, A., & Luckmann, T. 1989. *The structures of the life-world* (R. M. Zaner & D. J. Parent, Trans.), vol. 2. Evanston, IL: Northwestern University Press.

Scott, W. R. 1965. Reactions to supervision in a heteronomous professional organization. *Administrative Science Quarterly*, 10: 65–81.

Scott, W. R. 1987. The adolescence of institutional theory. *Administrative Science Quarterly*, 32: 493–511.

Scott, W. R. 2014. *Institutions and organizations: Ideas, interests and identities* (4th ed.). Thousand Oaks, CA: Sage.

Scott, W. R., & Davis, G. F. 2007. *Organizations and organizing: Rational, natural, and open system perspectives*. Upper Saddle River, NJ: Pearson.

Scott, W. R., & Meyer, J. W. 1994. *Institutional environments and organizations*. Thousand Oaks, CA: Sage.

Seidel, M.-D. L., & Greve, H. R. 2017. Emergence: How novelty, growth, and formation shape organizations and their ecosystems. M.-D. L. Seidel & H. R. Greve (Eds.), *Emergence. Research in the sociology of organizations*, vol. 50: 1–27. Bingley, UK: Emerald Publishing Limited.

Selznick, P. 1949. *TVA and the grass roots*. New York: Harper & Row.

Selznick, P. 1957. *Leadership in administration*. New York: Harper & Row.

Selznick, P. 1996. Institutionalism "old" and "new." *Administrative Science Quarterly*, 41: 270–277.

Sen, A., & Williams, B. 1982. Introduction: Utilitarianism and beyond. In A. Sen & B. Williams (Eds.), *Utilitarianism and beyond*: 1–22. New York: Cambridge University Press.

Shane, S. A., & Venkataraman, S. 2000. The promise of enterpreneurship as a field of research. *Academy of Management Review*, 25: 217–226.

Shapero, A., & Sokol, L. 1982. The social dimensions of entrepreneurship. In C. A. Kent, D. L. Sexton, & K. H. Vesper (Eds.), *Encyclopedia of entrepreneurship*: 72–90. Englewood Cliffs, NJ: Prentice-Hall.

Shipilov, A., & Gawer, A. 2020. Integrating research on interorganizational networks and ecosystems. *Academy of Management Annals*, 14: 92–121.

Sillince, J. A. A. 2005. A contingency theory of rhetorical congruence. *Academy of Management Review*, 30: 608–621.

Simmel, G. 1955. *Conflict*. New York: Free Press.

Simon, H. A. 1947. *Administrative behavior*. New York: Macmillan.

Simon, H. A. 1957. *Models of man*. New York: Wiley.

Simpson, B., & den Hond, F. 2022. The contemporary resonances of classical pragmatism for studying organization and organizing. *Organization Studies*, 43: 127–146.

Sine, W. D., & Lee, B. H. 2009. Tilting at windmills? The environmental movement and the emergence of the U.S. wind energy sector. *Administrative Science Quarterly*, 54: 123–155.

Slade Shantz, A., Kistruck, G., & Zietsma, C. 2018. The opportunity not taken: The occupational identity of entrepreneurs in contexts of poverty. *Journal of Business Venturing*, 33: 416–437.

Smets, M., Aristidou, A., & Whittington, R. 2017. Towards a practice-driven institutionalism. *The Sage handbook of organizational institutionalism*: 365–389. Thousand Oaks, CA: Sage.

Smets, M., Morris, T., & Greenwood, R. 2012. From practice to field: A multi-level model of practice-driven institutional change. *Academy of Management Journal*, 55: 877–904.

Smith, A. 1976. The theory of moral sentiments. In D. D. Raphael & A. L. Macfie (Eds.), *The Glasgow edition of the works and correspondence of Adam Smith, vol. 1: The theory of moral sentiments*. New York: Oxford University Press.

Smith, D. W. 2018. Phenomenology. In E. N. Zalta (Ed.), *The Stanford encyclopedia of philosophy* (Summer 2018). Stanford, CA: Stanford University. https://plato.stanford.edu/archives/sum2018/entries/phenomenology/.

Smith, L. T. 1999. *Decolonizing methodologies: Research and Indigenous peoples.* London: Zed Books.

Smith, W. K., & Besharov, M. L. 2019. Bowing before dual gods: How structured flexibility sustains organizational hybridity. *Administrative Science Quarterly*, 64: 1–44.

Snape, D., & Spencer, L. 2003. The foundations of qualitative research. In J. Ritchie & J. Lewis (Eds.), *Qualitative research practice: A guide for social science students and researchers*: 1–23. Thousand Oaks, CA: Sage.

Snidal, D. 2013. Rational choice and international relations. In W. Carlsnaes, T. Risse, & B. A. Simmons (Eds.), *Handbook of international relations* (2nd ed.): 85–111. Thousand Oaks, CA: Sage.

Snow, D. A., & Soule, S. A. 2009. *A primer on social movements.* New York: W. W. Norton & Company.

Somers, M. R. 1998. Symposium on historical sociology and rational choice theory "We're no angels": Realism, rational choice, and relationality in social science. *American Journal of Sociology*, 104: 722–784.

Sonenshein, S. 2010. We're changing – Or are we? Untangling the role of progressive, regressive, and stability narratives during strategic change implementation. *Academy of Management Journal*, 53: 477–512.

Soublière, J.-F., & Gehman, J. 2020. The legitimacy threshold revisited: How prior successes and failures spill over to other endeavors on Kickstarter. *Academy of Management Journal*, 63: 472–502.

Soublière, J.-F., & Lockwood, C. 2022. Achieving cultural resonance: Four strategies toward rallying support for entrepreneurial endeavors. *Strategic Management Journal*, 43: 1499–1527.

Soule, S. A. 1997. The student divestment movement in the United States and tactical diffusion: The shantytown protest. *Social Forces*, 75: 855–882.

Soule, S. A. 2009. *Contention and corporate social responsibility.* New York: Cambridge University Press.

Spee, A. P. 2020. *Elgar introduction to theories of social practice.* Northampton, MA: Edward Elgar Publishing.

Spee, P., Jarzabkowski, P., & Smets, M. 2016. The influence of routine interdependence and skillful accomplishment on the coordination of standardizing and customizing. *Organization Science*, 27: 759–781.

Star, S. L., & Griesemer, J. R. 1989. Institutional ecology, translations and boundary objects: Amateurs and professionals in Berkeley's Museum of Vertebrate Zoology, 1907–1939. *Social Studies of Science*, 19: 387–420.

Starbuck, W. H. 2003. Turning lemons into lemonade: Where is the value in peer reviews? *Journal of Management Inquiry*, 12: 344–351.

Steele, C. W. J., Hannigan, T. R., Glaser, V. L., Toubiana, M., & Gehman, J. 2021. Macrofoundations: Exploring the institutionally situated nature of activity. In C. W. J. Steele, T. R. Hanigan, V. L. Glaser, M. Toubiana, & J. Gehman (Eds.),

Macrofoundations: Exploring the institutionally situated nature of activity. Research in the sociology of organizations, vol. 68: 3–16. Bingley UK: Emerald Publishing Limited.

Stein, A. 1999. The limits of strategic choice: Constrained rationality and incomplete explanation. In D. Lake & R. Powell (Eds.), *Strategic choice and international relations*: 197–228. Princeton, NJ: Princeton University Press.

Stern, R. N., & Barley, S. R. 1996. Organizations and social systems: Organization theory's neglected mandate. *Administrative Science Quarterly*, 41: 146–162.

Stewart, A. 1989. *Team entrepreneurship*. Newbury Park, CA: Sage.

Stinchcombe, A. L. 1959. Bureaucratic and craft administration of production: A comparative study. *Administrative Science Quarterly*, 4: 168–187.

Stinchcombe, A. L. 1965. Social structure and organizations. In J. G. March (Ed.), *Handbook of organizations*: 142–193. Chicago: Rand McNally.

Stinchcombe, A. L. 1968. *Constructing social theories*. New York: Harcourt.

Stinchcombe, A. L. 1986. On getting hung-up and other assorted illnesses. *Stratification and organization*: 271–281. New York: Cambridge University Press.

Strang, D., & Soule, S. A. 1998. Diffusion in organizations and social movements: From hybrid corn to poison pills. *Annual Review of Sociology*, 24: 265–290.

Stuart, T. E., Hoang, H., & Hybels, R. C. 1999. Interorganizational endorsements and the performance of entrepreneurial ventures. *Administrative Science Quarterly*, 44: 315–349.

Stuart, T. E., & Sorenson, O. 2005. Social networks and entrepreneurship. In S. A. Alvarez, R. Agarwal, & O. Sorenson (Eds.), *Handbook of entrepreneurship research: Interdisciplinary perspectives*: 233–252. Boston, MA: Springer.

Swedberg, R. 2014. *Theorizing in social science: The context of discovery*. Stanford, CA: Stanford University Press.

Swidler, A. 1986. Culture in action: Symbols and strategies. *American Sociological Review*, 51: 273–286.

Tasselli, S., & Kilduff, M. 2021. Network agency. *Academy of Management Annals*, 15: 68–110.

Tavory, I., & Timmermans, S. 2013. A pragmatist approach to causality in ethnography. *American Journal of Sociology*, 119: 682–714.

Taylor, F. W. 1911. *The principles of scientific management*. New York: Harper.

Taylor, J. R., & Van Every, E. J. 2000. *The emergent organization: Communication as its site and surface*. Mahwah, NJ: Erlbaum.

Teece, D. J., Pisano, G., & Shuen, A. 1997. Dynamic capabilities and strategic management. *Strategic Management Journal*, 18: 509–533.

Thaler, R. H., & Sunstein, C. R. 2008. *Nudge: Improving decisions about health, wealth, and happiness*. New Haven, CT: Yale University Press.

Thompson, J. D. 1967. *Organizations in action*. New York: McGraw-Hill.

Thornton, P. H. 2004. *Markets from culture: Institutional logics and organizational decisions in higher education publishing*. Stanford, CA: Stanford University Press.

Thornton, P. H., & Ocasio, W. 1999. Institutional logics and the historical contingency of power in organizations: Executive succession in the higher education publishing industry, 1958–1990. *American Journal of Sociology*, 105: 801–843.

Thornton, P. H., Ocasio, W., & Lounsbury, M. 2012. *The institutional logics perspective: A new approach to culture, structure, and process*. New York: Oxford University Press.

Todd, Z. 2016. An Indigenous feminist's take on the ontological turn: 'Ontology' is just another word for colonialism. *Journal of Historical Sociology*, 29: 4–22.

Toubiana, M., & Zietsma, C. 2017. The message is on the wall? Emotions, social media and the dynamics of institutional complexity. *Academy of Management Journal*, 60: 922–953.

Tracey, P., & Phillips, N. 2016. Managing the consequences of organizational stigmatization: Identity work in a social enterprise. *Academy of Management Journal*, 59: 740–765.

Tsoukas, H. 2023. Afterword: Why and how phenomenology matters to organizational research. In F.-X. de Vaujany, J. Aroles, & M. Pérezts (Eds.), *The Oxford handbook of phenomenologies and organization studies*: 707–718. New York: Oxford University Press.

Tsoukas, H., & Chia, R. 2002. On organizational becoming: Rethinking organizational change. *Organization Science*, 13: 567–582.

Tsoukas, H., & Chia, R. (Eds.). 2011. *Philosophy and organization theory. Research in the sociology of organizations*, vol. 32. Bingley, UK: Emerald.

Überbacher, F. 2014. Legitimation of new ventures: A review and research programme. *Journal of Management Studies*, 51: 667–698.

Uzzi, B. 1997. Social structure and competition in interfirm networks: The paradox of embeddedness. *Administrative Science Quarterly*, 42: 35–67.

Uzzi, B. 1999. Embeddedness in the making of financial capital: How social relations and networks benefit firms seeking financing. *American Sociological Review*, 64: 481–505.

Vaara, E., & Whittington, R. 2012. Strategy-as-practice: Taking social practices seriously. *Academy of Management Annals*, 6: 285–336.

Vaitkus, S. 2000. Phenomenology and sociology. In B. S. Turner (Ed.), *The Blackwell companion to social theory*, vol. 2: 270–298. Malden, MA: Blackwell.

Vakili, K., & McGahan, A. M. 2016. Health care's grand challenge: Stimulating basic science on diseases that primarily afflict the poor. *Academy of Management Journal*, 59: 1917–1939.

Van de Ven, A. H. 1992. Suggestions for studying strategy process: A research note. *Strategic Management Journal*, 13(S1): 169–188.

Van de Ven, A. H. 2007. *Engaged scholarship: A guide for organizational and social research*. New York: Oxford University Press.

Van De Ven, A. H., & Johnson, P. E. 2006. Knowledge for theory and practice. *Academy of Management Review*, 31: 802–821.

Van Maanen, J. 1995. Style as theory. *Organization Science*, 6: 133–143.

Van Maanen, J., & Barley, S. R. 1984. Occupational communities: Culture and control in organizations. *Research in Organizational Behavior*, 6: 287–365.

Vasi, I. B., & King, B. G. 2012. Social movements, risk perceptions, and economic outcomes: The effect of primary and secondary stakeholder activism on firms' perceived environmental risk and financial performance. *American Sociological Review*, 77: 573–596.

Venkataraman, S. 1997. *The distinctive domain of entrepreneurship research.* In J. A. Katz & J. Brockhaus (Eds.), *Advances in entrepreneurship, firm emergence, and growth,* vol. 3: 119–138. Greenwich, CT: JAI Press.

Voegtlin, C., Scherer, A. G., Stahl, G. K., & Hawn, O. 2022. Grand societal challenges and responsible innovation. *Journal of Management Studies,* 59: 1–28.

Voronov, M., Glynn, M. A., & Weber, K. 2022. Under the radar: Institutional drift and non-strategic institutional change. *Journal of Management Studies,* 59: 819–842.

Voronov, M., & Vince, R. 2012. Integrating emotions into the analysis of institutional work. *Academy of Management Review,* 37: 58–81.

Waldinger, R., Aldrich, H., & Ward, R. 1990. *Ethnic entrepreneurs: Immigrant business in industrial societies.* Newbury Park, CA: Sage.

Walker, E. T. 2014. *Grassroots for hire: Public affairs consultants in American democracy.* New York: Cambridge University Press.

Walker, E. T., & Rea, C. M. 2014. The political mobilization of firms and industries. *Annual Review of Sociology,* 40: 281–304.

Wasserman, S., & Faust, K. 1994. *Social network analysis: Methods and applications.* Cambridge, UK: Cambridge University Press.

Weber, K., & Dacin, M. T. 2011. The cultural construction of organizational life: Introduction to the special issue. *Organization Science,* 22: 287–298.

Weber, K., & Glynn, M. A. 2006. Making sense with institutions: Context, thought and action in Karl Weick's theory. *Organization Studies,* 27: 1639–1660.

Weber, K., Heinze, K. L., & DeSoucey, M. 2008. Forage for thought: Mobilizing codes in the movement for grass-fed meat and dairy products. *Administrative Science Quarterly,* 53: 529–567.

Weber, M. 1930. *The Protestant ethic and the spirit of capitalism.* (T. Parsons, Tran.). New York: Scribner's.

Weber, M. 1949. *The methodology of social sciences.* (E. A. Shils & H. A. Finch, Trans.). Glencoe, IL: Free Press.

Weber, M. 1978. *Economy and society: An outline of interpretive sociology.* Berkeley, CA: University of California Press.

Weick, K. 2003. Enacting an environment: The infrastructure of organizing. In R. Westwood & S. Clegg (Eds.), *Debating organization: Point-counterpoint in organization studies*: 184–194. Malden, MA: Blackwell.

Weick, K. E. 1969. *The social psychology of organizing.* Reading, MA: Addison-Wesley.

Weick, K. E. 1979. *The social psychology of organizing* (2nd ed.). Reading, MA: Addison-Wesley.

Weick, K. E. 1988. Enacted sensemaking in crisis situations. *Journal of Management Studies,* 25: 305–317.

Weick, K. E. 1989. Theory construction as disciplined imagination. *Academy of Management Review,* 14: 516–531.

Weick, K. E. 1990. The vulnerable system: An analysis of the Tenerife air disaster. *Journal of Management,* 16: 571–593.

Weick, K. E. 1993. The collapse of sensemaking in organizations: The Mann Gulch disaster. *Administrative Science Quarterly,* 38: 628–652.

Weick, K. E. 1995. *Sensemaking in organizations.* Thousand Oaks, CA: Sage.

Weick, K. E. 1999. Theory construction as disciplined reflexivity: Tradeoffs in the 90s. *Academy of Management Review*, 24: 797–806.

Weiss, T., Eberhart, R., Lounsbury, M., Nelson, A., Rindova, V., et al. 2023. The social effects of entrepreneurship on society and some potential remedies: Four provocations. *Journal of Management Inquiry*, 32: 251–277.

Werner, T. 2012. *Public forces and private politics in American big business.* New York: Cambridge University Press.

White, H. C. 1981. Where do markets come from? *American Journal of Sociology*, 87: 517–547.

Whitford, J. 2002. Pragmatism and the untenable dualism of means and ends: Why rational choice theory does not deserve paradigmatic privilege. *Theory and Society*, 31: 325–363.

Whittington, R. 2003. The work of strategizing and organizing: For a practice perspective. *Strategic Organization*, 1: 117–125.

Whittington, R. 2006. Completing the practice turn in strategy research. *Organization Studies*, 27: 613–634.

Wicks, A. C., & Freeman, R. E. 1998. Organization studies and the new pragmatism: Positivism, anti-positivism, and the search for ethics. *Organization Science*, 9: 123–140.

Williamson, O. E. 1975. *Markets and hierarchies: Analysis and antitrust implications.* New York: Free Press.

Williamson, O. E. 1981. The economics of organization: The transaction cost approach. *American Journal of Sociology*, 87: 548–577.

Williamson, O. E. 1985. *The economic intstitutions of capitalism.* New York: Free Press.

Willmott, H. 2015. Why institutional theory cannot be critical. *Journal of Management Inquiry*, 24: 105–111.

Winter, S. G. 1988. On Coase, competence, and the corporation. *Journal of Law, Economics, & Organization*, 4: 163–180.

Woodward, J. 1965. *Industrial organization: Theory and practice.* London: Oxford University Press.

Wrege, C. D. 1986. The inception, early struggles, and growth of the Academy of Management. *Academy of Management Proceedings*, 1986: 78–88.

Wright, C., & Nyberg, D. 2017. An inconvenient truth: How organizations translate climate change into business as usual. *Academy of Management Journal*, 60: 1633–1661.

Wrong, D. H. 1961. The oversocialized conception of man in modern sociology. *American Sociological Review*, 26: 183–193.

Wry, T., Cobb, J. A., & Aldrich, H. E. 2013. More than a metaphor: Assessing the historical legacy of resource dependence and its contemporary promise as a theory of environmental complexity. *Academy of Management Annals*, 7: 441–488.

Wry, T., & Haugh, H. 2018. Brace for impact: Uniting our diverse voices through a social impact frame. *Journal of Business Venturing*, 33: 566–574.

Wry, T., Lounsbury, M., & Glynn, M. A. 2011. Legitimating nascent collective identities: Coordinating cultural entrepreneurship. *Organization Science*, 22: 449–463.

Wry, T., Lounsbury, M., & Jennings, P. D. 2014. Hybrid vigor: Securing venture capital by spanning categories in nanotechnology. *Academy of Management Journal*, 57: 1309–1333.

Yuchtman, E., & Seashore, S. E. 1967. A system resource approach to organizational effectiveness. *American Sociological Review*, 32: 891–903.

Yue, L. Q. 2015. Community constraints on the efficacy of elite mobilization: The issuance of currency substitutes during the Panic of 1907. *American Journal of Sociology*, 120: 1690–1735.

Zald, M. N. 1970. *Organizational change: The political economy of the YMCA*. Chicago: University of Chicago Press.

Zhao, E. Y. 2022. *Optimal distinctiveness: A new agenda for the study of competitive positioning of organizations and markets*. New York: Oxford University Press.

Zhao, E. Y., Fisher, G., Lounsbury, M., & Miller, D. 2017. Optimal distinctiveness: Broadening the interface between institutional theory and strategic management. *Strategic Management Journal*, 38: 93–113.

Zhao, E. Y., & Glynn, M. A. 2022. Optimal distinctiveness: On being the same and different. *Organization Theory*, 3: 26317877221079340.

Zhao, E. Y., Ishihara, M., & Lounsbury, M. 2013. Overcoming the illegitimacy discount: Cultural entrepreneurship in the US feature film industry. *Organization Studies*, 34: 1747–1776.

Zhao, E. Y., & Wry, T. 2016. Not all inequality is equal: Deconstructing the societal logic of patriarchy to understand microfinance lending to women. *Academy of Management Journal*, 59: 1994–2020.

Zietsma, C., Groenewegen, P., Logue, D. M., & Hinings, C. R. 2017. Field or fields? Building the scaffolding for cumulation of research on institutional fields. *Academy of Management Annals*, 11: 391–450.

Zietsma, C., Toubiana, M., Voronov, M., & Roberts, A. 2019. *Emotions in organization theory*. New York: Cambridge University Press.

Zucker, L. G. 1989. Combining institutional theory and population ecology: No legitimacy, no history. *American Sociological Review*, 54: 542–545.

Zuckerman, E. 2016. Optimal distinctiveness revisited. In M. G. Pratt, M. Schultz, B. E. Ashforth, & D. Ravasi (Eds.), *The Oxford handbook of organizational identity*: 183–199. New York: Oxford University Press.

Zuckerman, E. W. 1999. The categorical imperative: Securities analysts and the illegitimacy discount. *American Journal of Sociology*, 104: 1398–1438.

Zukin, S., & DiMaggio, P. J. 1990. Introduction. In S. Zukin & P. J. DiMaggio (Eds.), *Structures of capital: The social organization of the economy*: 1–36. New York: Cambridge University Press.

Index

academic freedom 102, 104
Academy of Management 3, 82, 89,
    104, 105
    Annual Meetings 107–8
    Organization and Management
        Theory (OMT) division 3, 80
Academy of Management Journal 3
Academy of Management Review 3
actions, instrumentally rational 31–2
actor network theory (ANT) 77
actors 50, 112
Administrative Behavior (Simon) 45
Administrative Science Quarterly 3
agency 77, 86, 91
Aldrich, H. E. 83, 84
Ansell, C. 5, 43
anti-corporate movements 57
arbitrage 101
arborescent assembling 113
assemblage theory 113
Association to Advance Collegiate
    Schools of Business (AACSB) 100
Astley, W. G. 12
Aston Group 39
Audia, P. G. 47
axiologies 7–8, 31, 44, 99, 114

Bain, J. S. 90
Barley, S. R. 69
Barney, J. 92
Becker, Gary 35
behavior, and relational ties 53
behavioral theory of the firm 45–8, 59,
    72, 94
bounded rationality 34, 45, 46

Bourdieu, P. 74
Brass, D. J. 52
Brewer, M. B. 96
Briscoe, F. 93
Bromley, P. 82
bureaucracy 15
Burrell, G. 5, 28, 61, 99
Burt, R. S. 53
business and management schools 3

Callon, M. 19, 33, 64, 76
Carnegie School 34, 45, 47
Carton, G. 77
categorization 96, 97
child labor 110
Christianson, M. 71, 72
Circuit Riders (social justice activists) 56
Clemens, E. S. 65
climate change 110
Clinton, Bill 110
Coase, R. H. 33
co-constitutive organization theories/
    theorists 15, 16, 19, 21, 59,
    61–79, 95, 112
collective mobilization 59
collegiality, in higher education 27
colonialism 6
competition 32
conflict 56
consumer watchdog field 56
contingency theory/theorists 11, 17,
    38–40, 49
contract law, and economics 91
Cooley, C. H. 65
Cornelissen, J. 73

Cosimo de' Medici 5
crowdsourcing 112
Crumley, E. T. 77
cultural change 56
cultural entrepreneurship 86–7
culture 20, 75
Cyert, R. M. 45, 46

D'Adderio, L. 96
Davis, G. F. 52
Davis, M. S. 24
decision-making 17, 22, 45, 72
    make versus buy 33–4, 91
    rational 32
DiMaggio, P. J. 67, 86, 87
distributed experimentation 112
Dreyfus, H. L. 62, 63
Duncan, R. B. 11
Durkheim, Emile 65
dynamic capabilities 92

economic forces 11
economic models 33
economics 76
    behavioral 35
    heterodox approaches to 89
    industrial organization 21, 91
    institutional 25, 33
    neoclassical 17, 32, 35, 45, 50, 52, 82, 89
    rational choice 18, 54
Economics of Strategy (Besanko) 89
economists, institutional 25
ecosystem services 30–31
Eisenstadt, S. N. 86
Elster, J. 31
embeddedness 85, 86
emergence, organizational 56
emotions, and institutions 69
enactment, theory of 50
engaged scholarship 21, 101–2, 114
Engelder, Terry 105–6
entrepreneurial groups 85–6
entrepreneurship 80, 81–8, 97
    cultural 86–7
    dynamics of 84
    emancipatory 88
    embeddedness approach to 86

institutional theory approaches to 86
Entrepreneurship Theory and Practice (journal) 82
environmental degradation 31
environmental movements 56
environmental uncertainty 11
epistemology 8
ethical coping 63
ethical skills 63
ethnic business growth 86
ethnomethodological approaches 14
European Group for Organization Studies 3
European scholarship 6

Feldman, M. S. 76, 96
Ferraro, F. 108, 111, 112
Follet, Mary Parker 19
Forestry Stewardship Council. 112
Foss, N. J. 83
fracking debate 105–6
Freeman, J. H. 35
Friedland, R. 68

Galileo 64
Gavetti, G. 46
Gehman, J 75, 86, 100, 105, 113
George, G. 108, 111
Giddens, A. 74
Glaser, V. L. 96
global financial collapse (2008) 33
Global Reporting Initiative 112
Glynn, M. A. 73, 87
Gond, J.-P. 76–7
grand challenges 21, 27, 30, 43, 107–14
Granovetter, M. 18, 42, 52–4
Greenspan, Alan 33
Greenwood, R. 77
Greve, H. R. 47, 94

Haack, P. 101
Hambrick, Don 104
Handbook of Organizations (March) 3
Hannan, M. T. 35
Hatch, Mary Jo 2
Hehenberger, L. 113

Heidegger, M. 63
Hernandez, M. 101
heterodox economic theories 25, 89
Hinings, B. 38
Hirschman, D. 61
Homo economicus 45, 64
Hoskisson, R. E. 89
human behavior 52–3
Husserl, E. 61, 63, 64
hydraulic fracturing 105–6
hyper-rationality 32

Ibarra, H. 54
ideal types 15, 113, 114
idealism 28
impactful theory 102
Indigenous scholarship 6
industrial organization 90
Ingraffea, Anthony 106
innovation 81
institutional entrepreneuring 113
institutional entrepreneurs 86
institutional logics 47, 68
institutional theory 19, 22, 64–70, 78,
    95, 96
institutionalization, of options trading
    markets 76
institutions, complexity of 69
intellectual property protections 109
isomorphism 67

Jarzabkowski, P. 75
Johnson, P. E. 101
Journal of Business Venturing 82

Ketokivi, M. 7
Khan, F. R. 110
King, A. A. 110
Klein, P. G. 83
Kuhn, T. S. 6, 7

Latour, B. 96
Lawrence, P. R. 39
Lawrence, T. B. 21, 22
legitimacy 50, 67
Leibenstein, H. 34
Lenox, M. J. 110

logics 47, 68
Lorsch, J. W. 39
Lounsbury, M. 47, 56, 68, 69, 77, 87

McGahan, A. M. 105, 109
McInerney, P.-B. 56
MacKenzie, D. 33, 76
Mair, J. 113
Maitlis, S. 71, 72
management 7
management theories/theorists 102
    applied 38
    classical 2, 19
managerial discretion 13
Mann Gulch fire 71–2
Mantere, T. R. 73
March, J. G. 3, 34, 38, 45, 46, 71, 72,
    111
Marti, E. 76–7
Mason, E. S. 90
materialism 28
Mead, G. H. 65
Merleau-Ponty, M. 62
Meyer, J. W. 66, 67
Meyer, R. E. 38, 66
Meyerson, D. E. 58
microeconomic theory 23
microeconomists 25
micro-macro linkages 81
Milliken, F. J. 11
Millo, Y. 33, 76
moral markets 56–7
morals 63
Morgan, G. 5, 7, 28, 61, 99
Morris, T. 77
multivocal inscription 112

Nelson, R. R. 91, 92
neoinstitutional theory 66
neopragmatism 18, 43
network theory 17, 85, 94, 95
networks 59
    embeddedness and 51–4
    social 52, 54, 85
new institutionalism 14, 65
nominalism 9, 10, 28
normativity 44

Obstfeld, D. 53
Ocasio, W. 47, 65, 68
Old Chicago School 69
ontological commitments 39–40
ontology 7, 9, 16, 20, 22, 27, 63, 114
    co-constitutive 54, 61
    and epistemology 8
    importance of 98
    pragmatic 42, 54, 55, 95
    rationalist 41, 82
    social 73
options trading markets 76
organization scholars
    courses taught by 103
    as teachers in business schools 100
Organization Studies (journal) 3
organization theorists, with robust
        scholarly identities 27
organization theory
    analogies in 7
    broad reach of 80–98
    contemporary 9–14, 99
    in entrepreneurship studies 82–8, 97
    mapping of 14–20
    overview of 2–9
    perspectives of 37
    societal impact of 102
    in strategic management 88–97
organizational behavior 12, 13
organizational ecology/ecologists 13,
        17, 23, 35–7, 40, 83
organizational environments 12, 49, 51
organizational institutionalism 65
organizational learning 48
organizations
    exogenous environment 29, 41
    interaction with suppliers, buyers
            and regulatory agencies 13
    life histories of populations of 36
    macro dynamics of the creation
            of 84
    relationship between context and
            structure of 39
    social interactions of 93
    as socially embedded 42
    viability of 40
Organizations (March & Simon) 46

Organizations in Action (Thompson)
        38
Orlikowski, W. J. 77

Padgett, J. F. 5, 54
Parsonsian tradition 20
participatory architecture 112
Pentland, B. T. 96
perception 62
performance feedback 47–8, 94
performativity 33, 76, 97, 102
permeability 102
Perrow, Charles 2
Pfeffer, J. 37, 49, 50
phenomenology 14, 19–20, 61–4, 78, 112
philosophy of science 6
Pillai, S. D. 94
population ecology 36
Porter, A. J. 112
Porter, M. E. 90, 92
poverty 88
Powell, W. W. 54, 67
power 49, 96
    episodic 21, 22
    market 21
    role in organization theory 21–2
    in sensemaking processes 73
    systemic 21, 22
practice, socio-materiality of 77
practice theory 19, 25, 73–8, 95
pragmatic theories/theorists 15, 18, 21,
        42–60, 111
    and entrepreneurial dynamics 84
    episodic power in 22
    philosophical foundations of 43–5
    rationalist theories and 58
pragmatism 18–19, 42
    American 43–5, 111
principal-agent problem 91
problem-solving 43, 44
*The Protestant Ethic and the Spirit of
        Capitalism* (Weber) 85
prototypical theories 16, 32
public engagement 105
public good 101
public intellectuals 104–7
public policy 101–2

Rao, H. 56
rational choice 17, 29
rational choice theories 29, 31–5, 58,
    64, 111
rationalist heterodox economic
    theories 89
rationalist theories/theorists 15–17, 22,
    29–41, 78, 79, 109
    contextual orientation of 29
    philosophical foundations of
        30–32
    power in 21
rationalized myths 67
realism 9–10, 28
reality 5, 101
Reckwitz, A. 74
recycling industry 56
Reed, I. A. 61
Reinecke, J. 102
Research in the Sociology of
    Organizations 3
Research Policy (journal) 82
resource dependence theory 48–51,
    57, 59
resource-based view (RBV) of the firm
    92, 94
resources 11, 109
Reus-Smit, C. 31
rhizomatic assembling 113
robust action 111–12
robust scholarly identities 5, 25, 27,
    99–115
Rorty, R. 43
routines 76, 91–2, 96
Rowan, B. 66, 67

Salancik, G. R. 49, 50
satisficing 34, 45
Schatzki, T. R. 74
Schildt, H. 73
Schneiberg, M. 57, 65
scholarly identities 4, 24–5
Schumpeter, J. A. 83
scientific concepts 64
Scott, W. R. 52
Scully, M. A. 58
self-interest 34, 35
self-regulation 110

self-restraint 31
Selznick, P. 13, 65
sensebreaking 71
sensegiving 72
sensemaking 19, 70–73, 78
Shapero, A. 85
Simmel, G. 51
Simon, Herbert 34, 45
skillful coping 62
Smets, M. 77
Smith, A. 32
social constructivist approaches 14
social dynamics 50, 58, 59
social enterprises 69
social justice activists 56
social movements 54–9, 93
social problems 100
The Social Psychology of Organizing
    (Weick) 70
social relationships 85
social structures 74
social theory/theorists 2, 3, 7, 12, 77
Sociological Paradigms and
    Organizational Analysis
    (Burrell and Morgan) 5
sociological scholarship 12
sociology 63, 80
Sokol, L. 85
Sorenson, O. 85
Soule, S. A. 57
Spee, A. P. 75
stakeholder theory 93
Steele, C. W. J. 69
Stinchcombe, A. L. 13, 65, 86
strategic management 17, 80, 81,
    88–97
strategy-as-practice (SAP) research
    75, 95
Stuart, T. E. 85
sustainable development 43–4

Taylor, J. R. 73
technology 81
tertius gaudens orientation 53
tertius iungens orientation 54
theoretical impact 102
theoretical packages 26, 27, 99
theoretical research communities 23–4

theories
  development of 23
  open-systems 8
  relationship between impact and
      101–2
  transfer of scholarly theories to
      practice 102
Thompson, James D. 38
Thornton, P. H. 47, 68
Toubiana, M. 69
transaction costs 33, 91
triads 51
trust 53

uncertainty 39
United Nations 67, 112
university governance 104
utilitarianism 17–18, 22, 30–32, 44,
    109

Vaara, E. 75
Vakili, K. 109
values 7, 63
Van de Ven, A. H. 12, 101
Van Every, E. J. 73

venture philanthropy 113–14
vertical integration 91

Waldinger, R. 86
Wang, M. W. 69
Weber, K. 56, 73
Weber, Max 12, 15, 31, 65, 85
Weick, K. 23, 50, 70–72, 78
Whittington, R. 75
Wiedenmayer, G. 83
Williamson, Oliver 33–4, 91
Winter, S. G. 91, 92
Woodward, J. 39
work, study of 69–70
world society theory 66
World Trade Organization (WTO) 109
Wry, T. 49, 50

X-efficiency 34

Zhang, C. M. 94
Zhao, E. Y. 96
Zuckerman, E. W. 97

Printed and bound by CPI Group (UK) Ltd, Croydon, CR0 4YY

23/04/2025

14660981-0001